The Guardian

CRYPTIC CROSSWORDS BOOK 4

Published in 2023 by Welbeck
An imprint of Welbeck Non-Fiction Limited
part of Welbeck Publishing Group
Offices in: London – 20 Mortimer Street, London W1T 3JW &
Sydney – Level 17, 207 Kent St, Sydney NSW 2000 Australia
www.welbeckpublishing.com

Puzzles © 2023 H Bauer Publishing
Design © 2023 Welbeck Non-Fiction,
part of Welbeck Publishing Group

Editorial: Millie Acers
Design: Bauer Media and Eliana Holder

A CIP catalogue for this book is available from the British
Library.

ISBN: 978-1-80279-429-8

Printed in the United Kingdom

10 9 8 7 6 5 4 3 2 1

The Guardian

CRYPTIC CROSSWORDS BOOK 4

A collection of more than **100** challenging puzzles

WELBECK

About the Guardian

The Guardian has published honest and fearless journalism, free from commercial or political interference, since it was founded in 1821.

It now also publishes a huge variety of puzzles every day, both online and in print, covering many different types of crosswords, sudoku, general knowledge quizzes and more.

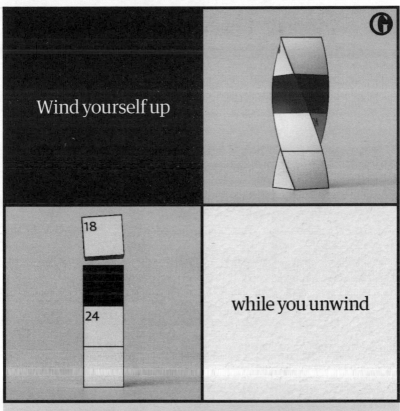

Introduction

Welcome to the fourth book in the *Guardian*'s brain-teasing puzzle series. The cryptic crossword puzzle has appeared in the pages of the *Guardian* for nearly a century, and these crosswords have been curated especially from recent issues to form a bumper batch of pure enjoyment.

Cryptic crosswords are one of the most perplexing puzzle types there are, but as a consequence they are also one of the most pleasing to solve. You will need linguistic skills, lateral-thinking abilities and plenty of patience to complete this book. The compilers have provided just enough clever clues to lead you to the right answer, but it will almost certainly take you some time to get there.

Above all though, please enjoy this book! The world is full of challenges, but we hope that these challenges will provide a delightful diversion for you.

Instructions

Set by Brendan

ACROSS

8 Semi-human creature Greek character encountered in youth (8)

9 In front of court, returned fire with maximal accuracy (5)

10 12 in place to practice for test (4)

11 Grand star risks changing into costume for South Pacific (5,5)

12 See 22

14 With paper around, secures floral decorations (8)

15,17 22 12 and regain selfpossession? (3,4,3,4)

20 Cheerful and not daft, consuming a half of stout (8)

22,12 9 19, or 4 25? (6,6)

23 Constant backer interrupting game (10)

24 22 in liquid, small well's contents? (4)

25 Equipment for performer absorbing us in this? (5)

26 Old weapon in framework had ugly appearance (8)

DOWN

1 Know-all I found on ocean in ragtag crew (8)

2 12 leading characters in Last of the Summer Wine, mostly (4)

3 Crone serving Americans food often accompanied by piped 25 (6)

4 Initially, Ronald Reagan represented order (7)

5 Daughter put in first green herbaceous plant (8)

6 Fast American runner or weightlifter, poor sportsman (10)

7 Moved to cellar, say, to put in second kind of wine (6)

13 Change layout of European newspaper in advance (10)

16 English team replacing head of business in crisis (8)

18 Person leaving vessel with one? Something used in kitchen (8)

19 For instance, certainly not turning over what should be cooled before serving? (7)

21 Party outside hotel, a lot of work? (2-4)

22 Bird is spotted when inside hide (6)

24 Placed around a 22 across, say (4)

Solution see page 249

Set by Vlad

ACROSS

1,13 In season? (7,2,3,5)

8 Able to supply Sainsbury's first, they vowed (7)

9 Groom takes look round capital (7)

11 The best time to work, setters say (3,4)

12 Movements of American singer unknown — is about to tour (7)

13 See 1

14 Rate working for police? Coppers quietly resigning (9)

16 Hope country girl's a sport — endless tease earlier (9)

19 Used bad language very loudly in centre of Leeds (5)

21 This is disappointing — you used to be sexy nurses (7)

23 Scary! It's flashing like a dirty old man (7)

24 Potter's equipment kept by artist (north countryman) (7)

25 Can't stand around outside Nancy's posh residence (7)

26 Ian presently sick but he may be rallying (6,6)

DOWN

1 Writer thought, 'Shut up!' (4,3)

2 Guide to China's ancient city (7)

3 Thing is, sweetheart, boss is busy working (9)

4 Exercise care carrying around bombs (5)

5 Did Nick check spaces in folder? (7)

6 Diamond's greatest hit in series? (4,3)

7 Cheeky artist's preparation for marriage (6,6)

10 Dominic tribute not popular — somehow it won't set a precedent (6,6)

15 Attic maybe calls for conversion, like this one inside (9)

17 Put on again for men in bar (female banned) (7)

18 Walked on both sides of road — noted repairs (7)

19 Royal family member nearly punching you once round mouth (7)

20 Picked up nude after driver's warning: 'Don't do it!' (7)

22 Can Tranmere Rovers finally get points? (5)

Solution see page 249

Set by Imogen

ACROSS

1 Aware of two men down (7)

5 Programme on TV that may support the Speaker (7)

10 Cut complaint that's expressed (4)

11 Hustling, sell us this leisurewear (5,5)

12 Old Roman company employing decorator (6)

13 In small segments, give out last message — fine, in fact (4,4)

14 Those fools are all ordinary people (3,6)

16 Credit turning round anti–British slogan (5)

17 Virginia houses some titled uncle (5)

19 Showing hammering: it's 7–0 (9)

23 Not one to lose argument, raised voice (8)

24 Promising to hold retreat, initially after a series of prayers (6)

26 Some peers are at this place, a dirty mess (10)

27 Run aboard huge vessel (4)

28 A belated idea to edit book of David's songs (7)

29 Fire out of control? Suppose not (7)

DOWN

2 Hotline fails, something from the Stone Age (7)

3 Shrink from cold, tucking into some alcohol (5)

4 They are missing food with pained expressions (2-5)

6 Youngster to switch positions over in place for drill (3,3)

7 Advantage for us sporting baggy clothes (4,5)

8 One third of trimester with head away, I get busy (2,3,2)

9 IoW feature last visited by people making maps of course (8,2,3)

15 Old American people get bigger: why not? (3,2,4)

18 Musical film shot in Oz (7)

20 Tragic figure not heading to French city in initial stages (5,2)

21 Dislike not having a translation (7)

22 With trouble, wife has endless long piece to iron (6)

25 Black book central to special offer(5)

Solution see page 249

4 Set by Picaroon

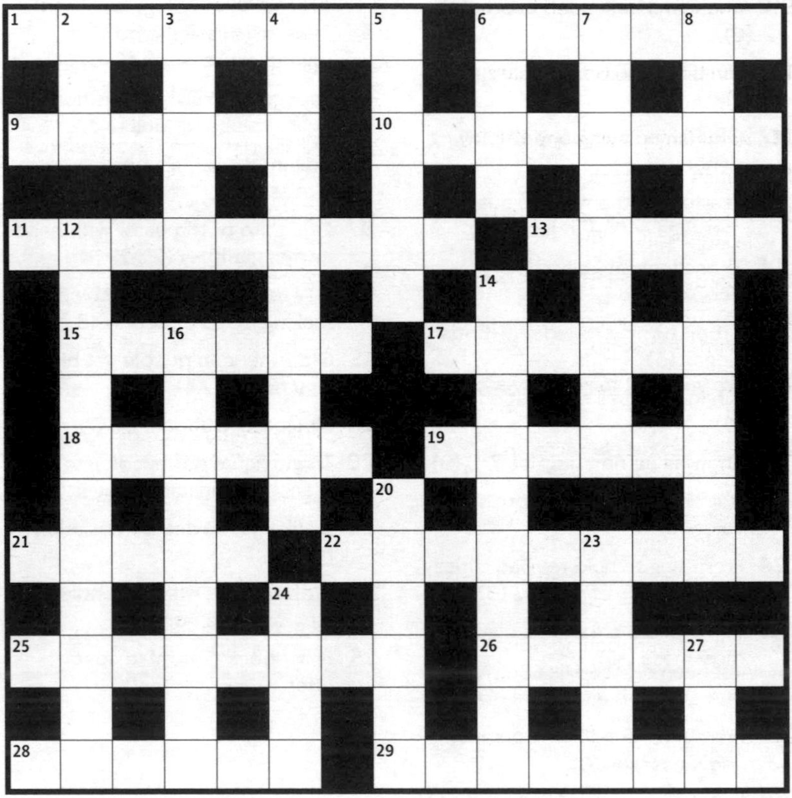

ACROSS

1 Bread stuffed with skin of guava for star 12 (8)

6 Something 12 which is played (6)

9 American 12 escaped heartlessly (6)

10 Men bound to be in uncle's place (8)

11 Actor isn't playing one 12 (3,6)

13 British pop star's activity 12 (5)

15 Double dose of salt for old invader (6)

17 Heard group of relatives is 12 (6)

18 Bets unclad singer is one making an impression (6)

19 Film star, fool taken in by fraud (6)

21 One's played character in Shakespeare play (5)

22 Show of preferences in walk nursing injured paw (5,4)

25 Perhaps saw advantage withdrawing money (4,4)

26 Place to park behind North American dressed like Batman? (6)

28 Church worker is to keep sending rude messages (6)

29 Revealing gear, things which are 12 (1-7)

DOWN

2 I get it's a sound made in mirth (3)

3 Single traveller's nose (5)

4 Lovingly taken home, lawman's clutching a tight back (10)

5 This person's job or duty (6)

6 Is 12 and isn't straight (4)

7 Well-liked people like me, who introduce extra pieces (9)

8 Golf games easily giving surge of emotion (11)

12 Untrustworthy? Then do field trips (2,3,6)

14 Performing carol, say, to event where Stradivarius has featured (5,5)

16 Call up troops, two officers besieging City (9)

20 Camp male's maintaining apparel on the outside (6)

23 He was 12 with some chap on zither (5)

24 Either end of Milton's poetic early period (4)

27 Girl who's 12? (3)

Solution see page 250

5 Set by Tramp

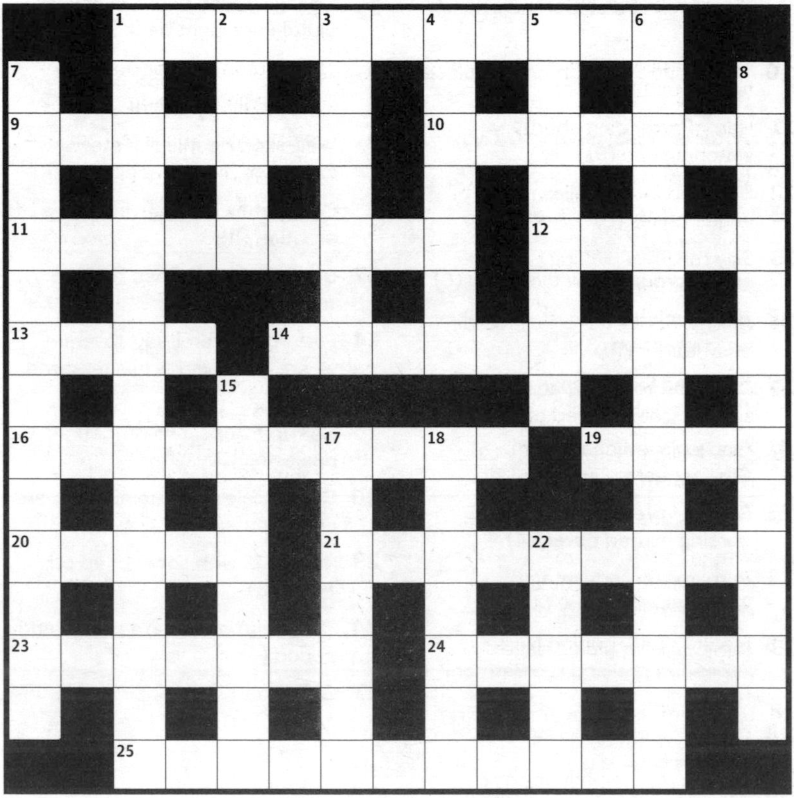

ACROSS

1 Order sponge that's cut or a piece of cake inside cafe (6,5)

9 Hospital patient's heart to pound; one in bed, perhaps is not so flat (7)

10 Drink running water with live newt further up (4,3)

11 Harry Potter cast shortly watching one (9)

12 Stopped in Australia, mostly at large houses (5)

13 Silly me loves writing puzzles after vacation! (4)

14 Cold-blooded American being busy leader (10)

16 Does one tend to watch hot girls soon to get stripped off (10)

19 Old designer leaving Italy to make scent for Americans (4)

20 Female, not in dresses, stuns (5)

21 With a better argument, American Mancini ultimately pens 'keep Moon River' (1,8)

23 Top journalist hiding page that's filled out (7)

24 Limited time to cut song during album set back (7)

25 Minor actor helping to win Oscar for project (11)

DOWN

1 Badger poacher with gun dealt reward at the end (6,9)

2 Live in sun during retirement (5)

3 Keep to right entering last passage (7)

4 Very neat in retrospect after biro's beginning to dry out (5,2)

5 Topless shoot that's red hot (4,4)

6 Region died: toxin released poisonous gas (8,7)

7 Massaging sporty hip, yeah? (13)

8 Film in April, May and June? (8,5)

15 Where desires are titillated by top-shelf bust (8)

17 Family man with pretty secretary (7)

18 Sign accordingly giving envelope for my foreign letter (7)

22 Arrival by alien going around Earth (5)

Solution see page 250

6

Set by Paul

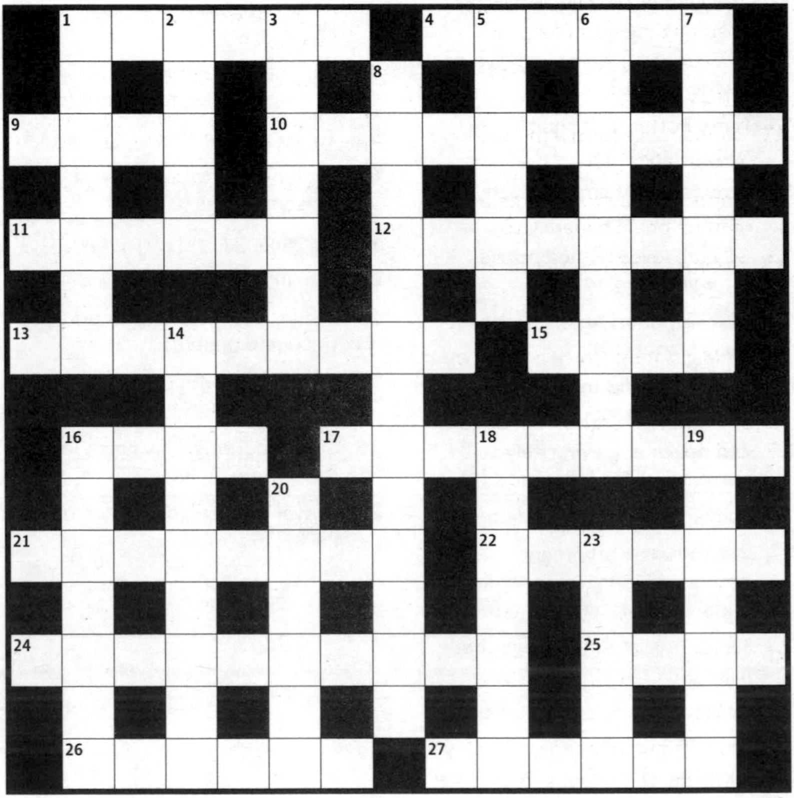

ACROSS

1 Race to eat a hot dog in America? (6)

4 See 27

9 Prayer an hour after midnight inspiring music, initially (4)

10 A picture forged: active safety measure (10)

11 Alpine rocks from a mountainous country (6)

12 Reportedly sudden surge of oil getting pan cleaner? (3,5)

13 Determination and spirit after first of defeats — one's beaten (5,4)

15,23 Might it be worth an offence in football? (4,5)

16,17 Paramour slightly off-centre? (1,3,2,3,4)

21 Present US president's a cow (8)

22 Magic of spring, might you say, in table of data? (6)

24 Longest of three years in penthouse, debauched (10)

25,20 Dope accessing superlatively exceptional region under threat (10)

26 Inadequate place to go in dirty dwelling (6)

27,4 Joined in action with mystical characters, those perhaps responsible for movement? (6,6)

DOWN

1 See 18

2 Start off bit before a dance (5)

3 A page worked in practical (7)

5 Grounds covered by area, so natural (6)

6 Awfully famous old picture? (9)

7 Upcoming clips about America in union (7)

8 Spruce in deep hole removed (4-6-3)

14 Long way after English, unknown Portuguese greeting French author (5,4)

16 A couple of affirmatives for primates (3-4)

18,1 Literary villain, one requesting a lift across northern suspension bridge, heading for trouble (7,7)

19 Worshipped, whether bound for heaven or hell? (7)

20 See 25

23 See 15

Solution see page 250

7 Set by Qaos

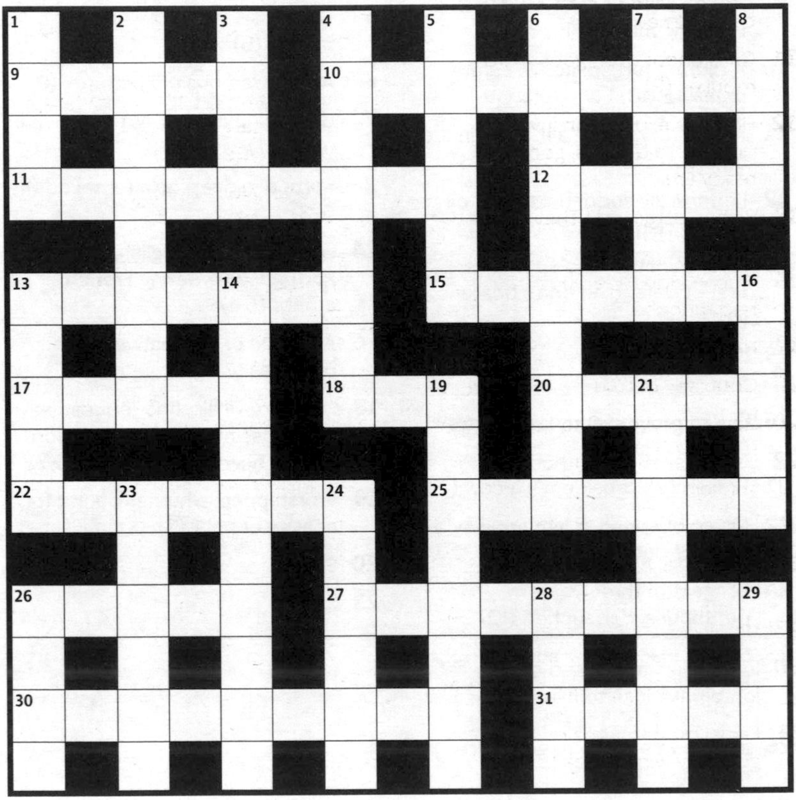

ACROSS

9 Modern, say, incorporating special style (5)

10 US labour leader, once topless, eating whipped cream when not being filmed (3,6)

11 Calls about oven get severe rebukes (9)

12 Homer's expression involves prelude to Ulysses, good and ready (5)

13 Bishop attacked? That's twisted (7)

15 Queen kidnapped by workers in bad moods (7)

17 Head to the end of 7 levels (5)

18 Criticise God (3)

20 How to go from 0 to 1 or 20? (5)

22 Leaves sections without model soldiers (7)

25 Man hides weapon in clothing (7)

26 British Rail now ruined by ex-PM (5)

27 Unfolded drapes, cryptically (9)

30 Ideas man lambasted guide over loo break close to five (9)

31 Facial preparations designed to get forty winks back (5)

DOWN

1 Commotion as difficult resit gets E- (4)

2 Dad ceased dancing outside as a stunt (8)

3 Copper's round, or is a square? (4)

4 Judge at home, immersed in dictionary, is happy being sophisticated (6-2)

5 Love very loud group's counterbalance (6)

6 No admirers swoon then die, perhaps (10)

7 Slim regularly, or need quiche (6)

8 #drugs? (4)

13 Book — what to do with it and what to buy it with (5)

14 Guarding posh spoiled girl tends to anger (10)

16 He's excited by Alien film (5)

19 Clothes to wear when you're out? (8)

21 Old writer — look down and be amazed (4-4)

23 Expert's against French art shows (6)

24 Smell bad in the Home Counties? Then wash! (6)

26 Black, black liquid swelling (4)

28 Good exercise channel (4)

29 Springfield was 80% clean (4)

Solution see page 251

Set by Pan

ACROSS

7 Attractive (male) doctor keeping old lady's back in good condition (9)

8 Nasty smell from yeast in kitchen (5)

9 Mixture of material made up of different substances used where builders work (9)

10 Pounds of British food (5)

12 Son never swimming in river (6)

13 Disturbance about Turkish leader in European parliament (8)

14 Couple suffering most woe (7)

17 Tradesman taking plane initially to timber (7)

20 Doctor wearing redder old hat (8)

22 Mostly stupid new Sunday exercises (3–3)

24 Place for special card (5)

25 Increase penalty in the end following misery initially at a Shetland winter festival (2,5,2)

26 Tin with old-fashioned tobacco (5)

27 Soprano interrupting tap dancing in polished comedy (9)

DOWN

1 Mat over hollow surface is wrinkled (6)

2 Captains fish in empty seas (8)

3 Strange numbers raised price in betting shop (4,2)

4 Demonstrate in favour of group returning to Thailand (7)

5 Master forced to group pupils by ability (6)

6 Case of sunstroke initially stopping nice tan developing (8)

11 Animal with large hood (4)

15 Big women going up and down on one leg (8)

16 People adopting independent manner (4)

18 Fish stew consumed in grotty motel (8)

19 Put together dish containing a bit of lemon to follow starters of chilled Ogen melon (7)

21 Support in reverse (4,2)

22 Travel guide translated phrase (6)

23 Spot, say, for fish (6)

Solution see page 251

Set by Vulcan

ACROSS

4 Most of broad hat is dark (6)

6 Paper not serious, but it's illuminating (8)

9 Given a pub meal, brought it all up (6)

10 In light footwear, turn and throw oneself down (4-4)

11 Waves to girl having to wheel herself along (6-5)

15 Meeting man in prison with sensitivity (7)

17 One army shattered: are there others? (3,4)

18 Be thoroughly malicious and toss one word out (2,4,5)

22 Where to see all sorts, from angels to zebras? (8)

23 XII, say, to cut out (6)

24 Insensitive, a singer working intensely (4,2,2)

25 An orderly area of the UK (6)

DOWN

1 Sort of block an easy task (6)

2 Grimaces — does more than tweak a nose! (5,1,4)

3 Awkward to walk on, like a light shoe? (8)

4 Take off in boat over region (8)

5 Spoil jewellery, adding mottled effect (8)

7 Legal arguments shortened festival (4)

8 Record that's broken at end of race (4)

12 For singer, maybe, arrange costume — it's to be altered (3,2,5)

13 Wooer captivates one lady-inwaiting (8)

14 Period when one learns fast? (4,4)

16 Councillor alarmed has to change name (8)

19 Getting larger waterproofing (6)

20 Wife remains clean (4)

21 Sound pleased to turn up with expensive motor (4)

Solution see page 251

ACROSS

8 Lack of talent not a feature of Lord's (8)

9 Flower shop online here? (6)

10 Foul-smelling old hat (4)

11 Short piece needing correction, with name for one composer finally changed (10)

12 Part of Manhattan, as far as two quarters will get you (6)

14 Name given to male deer, say? Originally, the ungulates in some faraway place (8)

15 Organised whole of largest alto section (7)

17 Veiled criticism of bargain gin supply (7)

20 Stupid people undone by this flaw? (8)

22 White chairs partially with designs using steel, glass and plastic, say (2-4)

23 Device that prevents pouring out of claret (10)

24 Nought drunk by small child? Just a little Coke (4)

25 Mum let sin get out of control (6)

26 Sadly risible, keeping Times owner's name inscribed in book here (2,6)

DOWN

1 Pass by failing to fail (8)

2 Bit of bacon some won't eat — rejected if not Danish, primarily (4)

3 Transported coal in another fuel container (6)

4 Rock night broadcast, with Yes playing first (7)

5 'Small beer' — second fellow's description of Miller's Willy (8)

6 Behind short film supporting revised rate for hearing aid (3,7)

7 Lines up outside No 10 — speech just beginning (6)

13 No longer called brother that's not working (3,2,5)

16 Attacked an idol with tie clip? That's 13 (4,4)

18 Cell deaths topped small number Puck's got cross about (8)

19 Fool includes certain guarantees (7)

21 Gripped by sudden fear, topless opponents in game lacking vital element (6)

22 Where kippers can be found on vacation in Harwich (6)

24 One form of pasta if potato, say, is short (4)

Solution see page 252

ACROSS

1 America backed Biden–Trump leadership election? At first, it's not obvious (6)

4 Substance affected Michael Caine's head (8)

9 Starts to 'accentuate the affirmative' gripping this poet (5)

10 Type of school for angling round at home (9)

11 Organising a relay run takes a bit over 50 weeks (5,4)

12 Not reactive or interactive (5)

13 Forking out to cover outrageous bill is charming (12)

17 Redundancy offensive involves only Conservative leader separately (12)

20 The 8 are about to change in Camberwell (5)

21 Right lane to turn one of us to strangers (9)

23 Digs up 12 butchered in Norfolk town (9)

24 Cutter's back at last with nickel and iron (5)

25 Boreal throne toppled by sailors (8)

26 In China, 2000 and 2012 are tedious (6)

DOWN

1 Telescope upset mostly Bohemian young woman (8)

2 British prince getting smarter (8)

3,8 Girl captivating girl with the dancing beams (5,6)

5 Event in which the murders end badly (7,6)

6 Fervent and overexcited about the central part of confessional (9)

7 My regularly acerbic major (6)

8 See 3

10 Summarily dismissed with this noise, lean out in panic (4,2,4,3)

14 Los Angeles Times editor's final hint about intricate passages (9)

15 Authentic ingénue's attractive (8)

16 Groom welcomes New Age colour (3,5)

18 Hideaway by river in London (6)

19 Does one leave a terrible bruise? (6)

22 Somebody who rambles for an hour about US president (5)

Solution see page 252

ACROSS

1 Forced to serve jam and egg crackers (5-6)

9 Stream barred return of predatory beast (7)

10 Artist and writer among group trying not to drink coffee, potentially (7)

11 Corps put faith in security (4,5)

12 False teeth regularly scrubbed fast (5)

13 Queen to withdraw for this reason? (4)

14 Highly awed seamen ran into harbours (4-6)

16 Rough sketches outlining germ warfare devices of 1940s (10)

19 Go out to lunch when retired (4)

21 Maybe sharper children worry (5)

22 Most brawny supplier in business grabs last of range (9)

24 False clone claiming ambassador's rank (7)

25 Fancy tie? Here's one in hand for Democrat to wear (7)

26 Inmate welcoming Oscar back after recital here? (7,4)

DOWN

1 Assembling, as partners may be, on green? (7,8)

2 Brilliant display mounted in oriental centre (5)

3 Handyman's powder spotted above shower (7)

4 Leaders in acoustics designed more suitable connector (7)

5 Unauthorised artwork revolutionary provided in strongly Labour newspaper (8)

6 Made mad excursion, when put off by everyone (6,2,3,4)

7 Mass publication (6)

8 Note-writer's favourable report on Simpson Jr? (6)

15 Case for money secured by First Lord of Admiralty primarily for small 12 (8)

16 Invoice in pouch-like holder, with penny change (6)

17 Dog's home supported by judge in Ulster (7)

18 Portable bed intended for nursery? (7)

20 Risk taken by fish shop (6)

23 Family lawyer of sorts? (5)

Solution see page 252

Set by Crucible

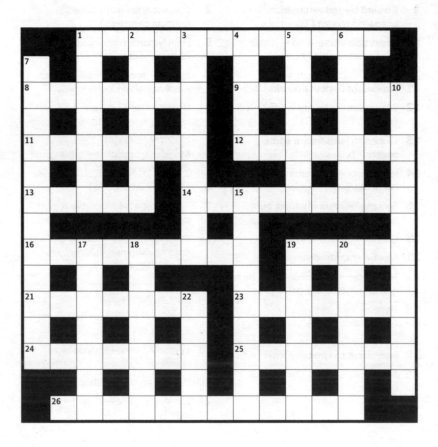

ACROSS

1 Order, say, two lots of aluminium with cheap bit thrown in (12)

8 Carried by sea westwards, third of team's missing coats (7)

9 Abandoned South American stopped ringing (7)

11 Trendy soldier's over visiting, notes swinger outside bar (3,4)

12 When swimming, plaice swallow gallons of ocean (7)

13 Work hard to acquire some essentially sexy allure (5)

14 Queen once has European hat back to front in part of UK (9)

16 Storyteller regularly read books in heart of Paris (9)

19 Children hand in tin (5)

21 Our neighbour's front replaced with first of painted struts (7)

23 A short distance divides Greek and Arab school (7)

24 Distance covered reversing, say, a cart (7)

25 Pen round old popular invention (7)

26 Cynic with dope and ale disrupted source of dope (12)

DOWN

1 A chum married Nimby, for one (7)

2 Issue one pound raised in merchandise (7)

3 Dimwit previously stole 'A New Feature of Poetry' (9)

4 Turn out to be the last to join in eastern party (3,2)

5 Remote city in ruins rebuilt (7)

6 African leader is circling a long time, twirling his weapon (7)

7 English team in large firm chart last of May and Johnson's work (12)

10 Some stars support speech, the result of 7 (12)

15 American wears fake top and army headgear (6,3)

17 Series covering last British king's mortification (7)

18 Workers collect delicious drink from this battered crate in city (7)

19 Flier, black one, blocks main road (7)

20 Motorists in Malta spoiled former capital (4-3)

22 Period working out in southern lakes (5)

Solution see page 253

ACROSS

9 Constitutional capital of Afghanistan twice (two) 14 (9)

10 As some boats flew, though not originally (5)

11 Party checked (5)

12 Help out, or fail to help children's author (2,4,3)

13 Empire behind supporter (7)

14 Capital of Lebanon twice bombed, returned to former glory? (7)

17 Capital of Norway twice 14 for birds (5)

19 Sign letter for the auditor? (3)

20 Block hiding other blocks (5)

21 Tango, then go for twist (7)

22 Get hot man — capital! (7)

24 One capital of France, twice 14, covering items (9)

26 Swollen stem: squash in roundabout (6)

28 Capital of Latvia twice 14 sought prize (5)

29 Briefly stir cream perhaps into strong coffee, creation of barista (4,5)

DOWN

1 Reportedly, break up exchange (4)

2 Able to bend, one held in place (6)

3 One capital of Spain twice 14, arranged by chance (10)

4 Capital author (6)

5 In the beginning, coat user shivering (2,6)

6 Capital getting up in the morning (4)

7 Time capital of Germany twice 14, more than 23, roughly speaking? (8)

8 Every second gone and rift opening underground (4)

13 Anything to eat ends in small hole for small predator (5)

15 Capital I would secure to invest in coffee (10)

16 Conveyed Theodore Roosevelt's letter opener? (5)

18 Eastern books on article in window (8)

19 Leave sign for musicians hosting upcoming meetings (5,3)

22 Again, relocate a US capital (6)

23 14, build new capital (6)

24 Call for paper (4)

25 Considered material (4)

27 Bird, tail by the ear? (4)

Solution see page 253

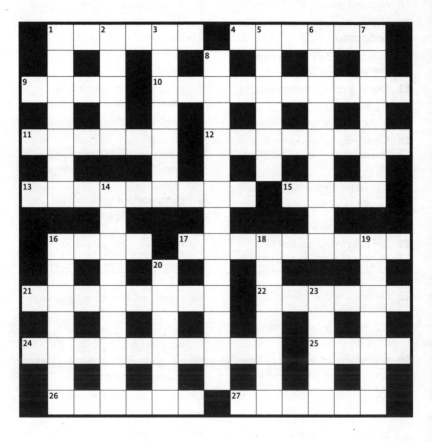

ACROSS

1 Revealed card is better (6)

4 Impede bad actor theatre rejected (6)

9 Lives with the French on Skye, perhaps (4)

10 Crib rails gape badly around infant's head (10)

11 Credit goddess for terrible situation (6)

12 Doctor taking fee cut (8)

13 Submission of plea involving Queen (9)

15 Name location on the radio (4)

16 Playful piece of music lacking intro (4)

17 Meet religious group to the east of Bury (9)

21 Piano and stringed instrument returned by worker complaining (8)

22 Go by plant (6)

24 Meticulous firm promises to hide identity (10)

25 Warning from heads of Ofsted mentioned extra numeracy (4)

26 Lucrative work student left out (6)

27 Agreement from number overwhelmed by strength (6)

DOWN

1 Watch old boy wait (7)

2 Lock theatre's spare boxes (5)

3 Progress hampered by setter repeatedly leading to deadlock (7)

5 A dish church gives to each individually (6)

6 Pictures left by artist having oddly deficient vistas (9)

7 Prize setter trotting around ring (7)

8 Lobby people to accept unlimited lucid dream (13)

14 Leaderless troops oppose battle (9)

16 Over time, state becomes mean (7)

18 Displays old models (7)

19 Kind of glue covering bottom of label (7)

20 Worker left European stock (6)

23 Press release on individual is lying (5)

Solution see page 253

Set by Pasquale

ACROSS

1 That moralising upset numbers in old-fashioned school lessons (14)

8 Quiet refuge for animals and fish (5)

9 Attractive home — paying a call is not permitted (8)

11 Like some bought items with quiet salesman to help (7)

12 Friendly Queen knocking one out as usual (7)

13 Some relief if there's a musical interval (5)

15 Artist with Welsh name who transformed old entertainment (5-4)

17 Mistake with awkward bust, female finally squeezing into these? (4,5)

20 Old police force, given its situation, about to suffer (5)

21 Yesterday's religious leaflet or a passage from it? (7)

23 Energy-packed tea with cooked item — it's not expensive (7)

25 I need job done ... (3,5)

26 ... to eclipse my predecessor (5)

27 Financial document provided by three characters joined in impecuniousness (10,4)

DOWN

1 Feel boas and asps get nasty in old stories (6,6)

2 'Card' as someone who might pull your leg? (5)

3 Without hesitation, fate has sealed ex-president as initiator of hatred (4,1,4)

4 Smile, looking embarrassed, showing up tooth (7)

5 Partygoer stealing silver is one causing much damage (7)

6 Big person to get screwed up, we hear? (5)

7 Head of state's icon, working with charm (9)

10 Hippies quietly elope, running south of river? (6,6)

14 Father on time to meet party men in entrance to house? (5,4)

16 Very gradually start off to conceal excavation (9)

10 Before Caesar's last day something risky happens (7)

19 Musical part that you get with Prokofiev but not with Mendelssohn (7)

22 A seat occupied by Liberal — is this a record? (5)

24 Greek philosopher half ignored old Roman god (5)

Solution see page 254

ACROSS

1 Saw fewer people in business (7,7)

9 Pilot participating in raid and a rescue (3,4)

10 Refuse cold chop sent back for demanding chap (7)

11 Something hot? The opposite when picked up (5)

12 Love a portion sliced by cook (9)

13 Denies president's hosting new billionaire (9)

14 Tory grandee's hot with fever (5)

15 Bear first sign of tailspin (5)

17 Passage of a good king, dressed with flourish (9)

20 Ponders brief massage — setter's back and bum! (9)

22 Head of patriotic state who puts out flags (5)

23 English prompt to store wood in rural work (7)

24 Experience high oil supply from this city? (7)

25 Thug about to stop washing pants (5,9)

DOWN

1 Boy and unknown person talking on line, a seeker of romance (4,10)

2 Two males welcoming one making a pile (7)

3 Drink alone in a provocative way (9)

4 Moulded terse version of Caesar's Rubicon speech? (3-4)

5 Weighty responsibility saving deposit up (7)

6 Red paper out of very fashionable company (5)

7 Love alcoholic drink that's kept diluted (7)

8 Dreamboat preparing to hug dissolute chancer (6,8)

14 Gyrating hip, thong covering one's best part? (4,5)

16 Demi Moore's outside with grand French film-maker (2,5)

17 Maybe Rosemary's Baby's opening after fuss (7)

18 Dry wine European bottles getting badge of honour (7)

19 Where air's kept awfully volatile after temperature drops (7)

21 Edible plants raised by Nile's banks in arid area (5)

Solution see page 254

Set by Boatman

ACROSS

1 Following report of communist, letters must show these (9)

6 Suffer no fool: Canute misquoted about heresy, initially (4)

8 Decreed: set gold before man of the North, reported journalist (8)

9 Old heartless Richard III in feud about filth (6)

10 Stand for leadership of the youth party in free Yugoslavia (6)

11 Gave out (caught), left in, left out (8)

12 Way a man embraces a queen (6)

15 Renovated seediest part of the North (8)

16 As at first, Henry VIII was intellectual (8)

19 In Scotland's valleys, Elizabeth's heart picks up (6)

21 Plot to murder princes about nothing (8)

22,1down Terrible danger, with political activists at Buckingham House event (6,5)

24 Man of the North, as James I was in Scotland! (6)

25 Boatman, at heart European, in first part of Tory attack (4,4)

26 Charles broadcast to listeners? (4)

27 Lorry then diverted in the direction of Scotland? (9)

DOWN

1 See 22 across

2 Perhaps Victoria is not at fault (7)

3 Unwashed masses taking king's head (5)

4 Alfred: he atoned partly for the result of a fire (3,4)

5 Snack in foil, say pig's foot (6,3)

6 Edward, our sovereign, showed passions (7)

7 King, to be beheaded, takes sanctuary somewhere near Wembley (9)

13 Oh, I parted sadly from love's image (9)

14 Exercising restraint, as the Queen is said to do in spirit (7,2)

17 More unpleasant than retsina? Unlikely! (7)

18 Getting bigger, King George: one defined by his appetite? (7)

20 Boatman placed between noble and royal persons previously (7)

22 Harold at first confessed rising up to snap in anger (5)

23 Good to leave the upper class no way out (5)

Solution see page 254

Set by Paul

ACROSS

7 I'm fed up with the wet country (7)

8 American drink in French house (7)

9,21down Spooner's man with a beard in prayer? (4,4)

10 Gone to collect windcheater, finally given a coat (9)

12 Notice rifle shot (5)

13 Pay people running competition? (4,4)

15 Range one voluntarily holds back (4)

16 A tree drops on author (5)

17 See 5

18 Taken before lunch, stuff including black seafood (8)

20 Creation of 16 across in shade of tree? (5)

21 Measure of cycles is very painful, reportedly? (9)

22 Bloke having lemon sole in the end (4)

24 Space vacated after journey including a trek (7)

25 See 6

DOWN

1 Spanish drink — it's okay for the French (4)

2 Singin' about a creation of 16 across (8)

3 Creation of 16 across, money (6)

4 Make bombs to defend old game (8)

5,17across A day daughter enters payment for creation of 16 across (6,4)

6,25 Creation of 16 across, cross monitor (4,7)

11 Telescope on, characteristic rings appear, ultimately (9)

12 Creation of 16 across, money (5)

14 Note obsessive passage (5)

16 Purple: the mast after rigging containing hint of yellow (8)

17 Almost twelve taking lift became unconscious (5,3)

19 Creation of 16 across head honcho (6)

20 Risk a couple of sharp bends, challenging corners (6)

21 See 9

23 Avoid cricketing failure (4)

Solution see page 255

Set by Brendan

ACROSS

8 For middle of month, put in one unknown soldier, historically (8)

9 Back a time and a place for events (5)

10 Dramatically it follows the winter's end, we hear (4)

11 Some February mail — around middle of month lets naive get excited? (10)

12 Springtime festival's call for help (6)

14 British admitting poet wanting to return in April (8)

15 Be scrupulous with slight touch after start of summer (7)

17 March, perhaps, for international event (7)

20 Said with relief where royalty goes in summer sometimes (8)

22 Saint seen in one page of annual publication? In a way that's fair (6)

23 Frantically organises to contain end of spring hostility (10)

24 Stretch between spring and end of autumn (4)

25 Our group on board? Reduced fare from Japan (5)

26 Specimens one removed from tall buildings after test (8)

DOWN

1 Cause of cloudiness that affects visibility in fall (8)

2 Help for speaker that comes before November (4)

3 Heart specialist's trick taking in Republican on the Fourth of July (6)

4 Information on courses, some tribally set up (7)

5 You can't miss it on board at sea before year's end (4,4)

6 Names dynasty one's located among offspring being raised (10)

7 Oktoberfest setting for local by replacing TV, bit by bit, in pub (6)

13 Russian revolutionary's exceptionally discreet about doctor (10)

16 Test ground with it, as rule (8)

18 Violently attacked about pound being rescued (8)

19 Upset last month over mail being misdirected, it's asserted (7)

21 A flurry about Burmese title that's imposing (6)

22 Place in Alaska where gold's found after start of summer (6)

24 Short part of year for some Irish clan (4)

Solution see page 255

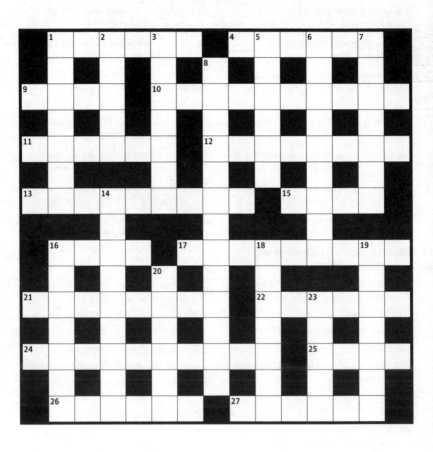

ACROSS

1 Proudly show off row of shops (6)

4 Sponge ass's back — pleased expression (6)

9 To express disapproval of Mike leads to explosion (4)

10 Greek character nothing short of brave and gallant (10)

11 Tell why one is playing well (6)

12 Getting washed and dressed: after work, better to avoid extremes (8)

13 Doing really well with a spreadsheet? (9)

15 Read endlessly as boss (4)

16 Get rid of bed (4)

17 Approve art house I rebuilt (9)

21 In bodies a judge addresses damages (8)

22 Waddle half back, and don't hurry (6)

24 Loud than a storm at sea? That's lucky (4,2,4)

25 Called up to manage golf (4)

26 New weapon is limited (6)

27 Resolve to belt criminal (6)

DOWN

1 Mythical bird? It's found in Arizona (7)

2 Capital lover and capital love (5)

3 Counting system with a point to it (7)

5 Giraffes' cousins fine, needing a short wee (6)

6 Hot meal for this circus artiste? (4-5)

7 Searched round area frequently visited (7)

8 Eminent inspector with poor suiting dropped (13)

14 After short space nobleman and monarch meet (9)

16 Painful experience after bathing? (7)

18 Spanish gentleman concealed goal stupidly (7)

19 Something considered golden is shut up (7)

20 As if alternative company could be a complete disaster (6)

23 Poorest quality terrace put up on street (5)

Solution see page 255

ACROSS

1,15 Legend, very generous sort, Mrs Thatcher — as if! (6,9)

5 One's appeal right for inspiring artist (8)

9 12 flipping thick, Lewis Hamilton now said (8)

10 Not totally wanton, I'm saying about woman (6)

11 Initially nervous: when turning to drink, gains a little extra confidence (12)

13 Shock for a criminal (4)

14 Idiot's taken in twice about countryman (8)

17 Canister could be smaller (8)

18 Was sorry about making vulgar sound (4)

20 Bar staff finally on site dressed as pirates (12)

23 Lawyer with German's money getting in bother (6)

24 One being spiteful about letter going too far (1,3,4)

25 Associates with right–wing types (8)

26 Close to rock, gets to swim with a seal (6)

DOWN

2 Insatiable drama queen stood up (4)

3 Easily passes with professor coming round (5,4)

4 Queen's in study endlessly drinking alcohol (6)

5 Increasingly disconcerted by standards in war novel (in more than one way, some might say) (3,3,4,5)

6 Declare — Lara heading off after leg bye (8)

7 Wrongly firing Minister without Portfolio at first (5)

8 Brings back some method of control over Washington? (10)

12 An oaf at first implying Covid not very problematic — nut! (10)

15 See 1

16 Awful rubbish! Charlie upset person calling the shots (8)

19 Weakness with fellow off sick (6)

21 Labels men as fickle (5)

22 After not much revision, came top (4)

Solution see page 256

Set by Qaos

ACROSS

9 1 + 50 + 1 = 1? (5)

10 Around 4, take out the person responsible (9)

11 Unhappy about eating hot sauce, company leaves European record stores (9)

12 Orders strong cheese to start with (5)

13 Leader's fitting in the third person (7)

15 Put back in forest or earth (7)

17 John who lives in a Cambridgeshire village (5)

18 Short boy skipped half of class (3)

20 Around Reading, one's selling fish (5)

22 Excited to be in expensive car with cigarettes (4–3)

25 Cracked porcelain? No, no, it's a copy (7)

26 Amazing soldier enters river doing a backflip (5)

27 Carbon, hydrogen and metals: I turn them into gold (9)

30 Mocking learner after Day One — car breaks down around lunchtime (9)

31 Queen wears hat regularly for courage (5)

DOWN

1 Outlaw finally joined gang (4)

2 Weakness for very loud ties, at first turning heads (4,4)

3 Partner following him? A plant (4)

4 For each issue, one pound for an ad (8)

5 They say London bloke often spouts a lot of hot air (6)

6 British pub rebuilt as junkyard (7,3)

7 Adult 1 — child 0 in martial art (6)

8 Dispute amount to pay Britain in recession (4)

13 King Charles initially leads without difficulty (5)

14 New nurse cannot take temperature for newsreaders (10)

16 Old method to lift up more (5)

19 Zappa's commercial album? Absolutely (8)

21 Nothing in a girl's novel is creative (8)

23 From beginning to end, cut crossword solutions (6)

24 It's uncommon for society to worry about carbon (6)

26 Bond's boss to query disguise (4)

28 Response from online church — 'love' (4)

29 Shabby articles by English gallery (4)

Solution see page 256

ACROSS

1 Young Bengal tigers skirting lake? They're used to exercise (6,5)

9,10 The hardest thing before match — it's achieved years later (7,7)

11 Large-scale course briefly a focus for seismologist (9)

12 Continental banker, extremely rich individual (5)

13 Flipping insect bite! (4)

14 Declared start of amnesty during forecast (10)

16 Singles-only holiday? (3-3,4)

19 Unladen long-range spaceships taking off (4)

21 Mammal (un)like fawn (5)

22 Hardy female graduates framing article about mum (9)

24 Parisian who joins the marines aboard feels awkward (7)

25 One's played two blues oddly rejected by British university (7)

26 Pass card to successor, swearing? (4,2,5)

DOWN

1 Lastly, shake anti-viral fluid before opening it (7,8)

2 Queen's mate cheated, taking queen in (5)

3 Examiner's car upset bull (7)

4 Chicken he brought in for a farmhand (7)

5 Play with reserve, in accordance with law (8)

6 21 run off in pursuit of junk shop thief (4,2,3,6)

7 Commercial dressings primarily frustrate nurses (6)

8 A European king's missing daughter's OK (6)

15 Aged Scots in hag's bottomless cooking pot? (8)

16 General charges with sergeant perhaps to stop army heading off (6)

17 Hot sauce, like cold, served in fancy bout (7)

18 Where Naomi's tale's told — about time, really (2,5)

20 Bill's rushed round, forcibly removed from ground? (6)

23 Adult in blazer needing a bath (5)

Solution see page 256

25 Set by Paul

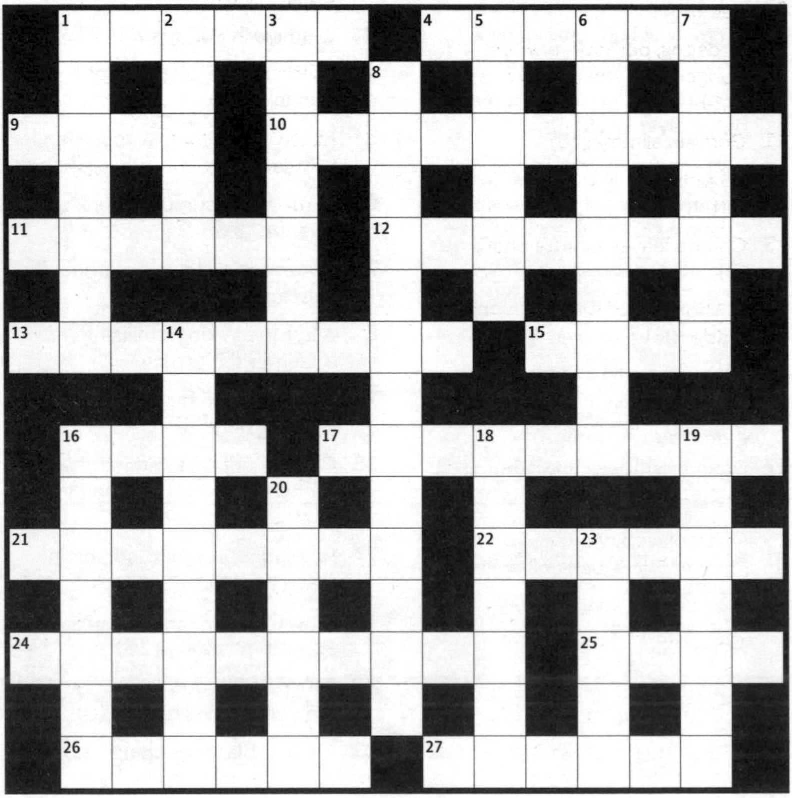

ACROSS

1 Fine under hat, one invisible (6)

4 Brand magistrate crooked after waiving of charge (6)

9 See 19

10 Birdsong, perhaps, in worst dungeon, by the sound of it? (4,6)

11 German slimmer (6)

12 US politician in priest turned rotten (8)

13 Champ leaves hirsute character (9)

15,18 Those contraptions would judder as he worked aboard loco (11)

16,5 One enjoying a drink eats nuts in season (10)

17 Dimmer student finally admitted to county town after pretty low grade (3,6)

21 Numbers coming up, split spoils including deposit (8)

22 Foreign helper in middle of room, might you say? (2,4)

24 Measure girl, OK after reviewing contrary novel (10)

25 Book search in Birmingham? (4)

26 Work out the other royal title (6)

27 Behind schoolmaster, necking drinks (6)

DOWN

1 European vegetable's ending in Cornish pasty, possibly? (7)

2 Tool securing unloaded device behind washer (5)

3 Country in deceit more fuelled by alcohol, reportedly? (7)

5 See 16 across

6 Medicine served up in prison, one in disastrous campaign (9)

7 Round rings, circle left in region on base of nipple (7)

8 What man in essence and woman in effect both have proverbially to solve the problem immediately? (1,6,2,4)

14 Result of pat on baby's back, turn remarkably soppy (9)

16 Cryptic was like exercise for setter, say? (7)

18 See 15

19,9 Small potatoes or peanuts, nibbles for hen party? (11)

20 Enter king, say, carrying head of Republican (6)

23 Seed perhaps mine, though not a tree, ultimately (5)

Solution see page 257

ACROSS

7 Rubbish kisser's naughty coming first (8)

9 Start of FedEx round, flipping overdue: like someone awaiting delivery? (6)

10 Boxing match, essentially with star sees knock out (4)

11 He left a fluid around badger's home: they might come out at night? (5,5)

12 Chest tender following cold (6)

14 Churchmen with energy at the start: they can lift an organ (8) 15 Stupid person put on island (6)

17 A lot of McDonald's milk products on the turn (6)

20 Most difficult son with ultimate challenge (8)

22 Gorge in do to welcome in a New Year (6)

23 Rose more sick swallowing a tablet? (10)

24 Pad of paper with note written inside (4)

25 Love saucy thing (6)

26 Work out sum, learn figures (8)

DOWN

1 Diet of mostly odd junk? (4,4)

2 Signal with no hands (4)

3 One on internet is more confident around female (6)

4 Swear on English TV heartlessly in a way that's weak (8)

5 American president awfully boring (10)

6 One takes orders from one wearing hose (6)

8 Joining hospital not as new case (6)

13 Repeatedly in fear? Thing will ultimately get chewed (10)

16 Seeing curvy figure providing cover for OK! (8)

18 Make love and left partner crazy (8)

19 Taken to beer without opening tin cans (6)

21 Tablet around midnight? Date getting high (6)

22 Hour in deep sleep showing quality of shade (6)

24 Axe tree down to earth (4)

Solution see page 257

ACROSS

4 Tamper with retro piece of religious iconography outside court (6)

6 Plant found by fish next to part of canal network (8)

9 Medical emergency caused by a speaker's inactivity (6)

10 Slope in garden altered to accommodate one plant finally (8)

11 Fruit with extremely likeable fragrance has a fine lustre (11)

15 College head leaves part-time judge to request another delivery (7)

17 Huge flow of gold found in British river (7)

18 Wise men given no time to join those waiting to see old French fortifications (7,4)

22 Sharp fielder catching good new Australian (8)

23 Relative trapping animal in bottle (6)

24 Court official with gratuities for office workers (8)

25 Reflect, as young person runs for navy (6)

DOWN

1 Small piece of mushroom without top of stalk (6)

2 Dance, though Rachel and son not dancing (10)

3 Aggressor's press release to editor returning duty list (8)

4 Return said sources of 3, 7, 15 and

9 for all those who have left their homeland (8)

5 Drama changed into half comedy for produce some spice (8)

7 Old writer in annual golf event (4)

8 Bird originally kept in tiny enclosure (4)

12 Dish of beef roast, carved up with good source of nutrients, is no longer on the menu (10)

13 Creative type's gender is fluid (8)

14 Flag flown by ship crossing river (8)

16 Two notes put away following Norway leader's command (8)

19 Very sad soldier in vehicle going back uphill (6)

20 Covers over notice (4)

21 Detective in touch with politician's solicitor (4)

Solution see page 257

Set by Brummie

ACROSS

8 Seeming to turn old man against old man? (8)

9,2 Cheap wedding ring that plays tunes (5,4)

10,25 Sweet things like to embrace detectives and dribble (4,5)

11 Understanding exercise function requires no energy (10)

12 Crossword started (bloody Brummie!) — time to have belief (6)

14 Bedding etc unfortunately restricts active lover (8)

15 Get high on your own smart performance (3,4)

17 Sediment area around house (7)

20 Bird's bill, cornet-shaped (8)

22 Having a particular way of removing outer bits from crusty larvae (6)

23 Britten composition found inside Bird's plant (10)

24 Chamber is consequently filled by island lake (4)

25 See 10

26 Withdraw, carrying emptied rifle, being cowardly (8)

DOWN

1 Insubstantial small muscle lacks oxygen (8)

2 See 9

3 Desirable person's improper message about urine container (6)

4 Appeal to leaders of African tribal region (7)

5 Round book printed on dedicated computer paper (8)

6 Is the Queen unable to cover an old music stand? (10)

7 Wood and metal off the boat (6)

13 Analysis of Pluto zone (10)

16 Affectedly well-read, or else excited about it (8)

18 Unmissable date — and phone not working? (8)

19 University, rather unorthodox, that's used by a peer (7)

21 Dull city centre's gone flashy inside (6)

22 Swipe church sample (6)

24 Lacking source of education, looks up 'beehive' (4)

Solution see page 258

ACROSS

1 Mineral brought down, said Pole (8)

6 Delegate's record in service (6)

9 Faith very receptive to suggestion (6)

10 Selector's remarkable piece of armoury (8)

11 In the last month in college, apply to do lots together (9)

13 Religious celebration fixed around 2nd February (5)

15 Put up with a lecturer from the north (6)

17 Some may say sex worker has a stout rope (6)

18 What one may hear from horse thief (6)

19 Owns toboggan, endless bother (6)

21 Refuse to vote for 13 (5)

22 Pastry not very short, value doubtful (3-2-4)

25 In search for compliments maybe, always a bit frenzied (8)

26 A little fluid, say, not a condition full of it (6)

28 Really enjoyed a party, looking flushed (6)

29 Death — by hanging? (8)

DOWN

2 An old letter from Goethe (3)

3 Snack one's left to boil over (5)

4 Racing driver considered to have gone flat out (10)

5 Announce as unsuitable function of playground (6)

6 Died on boat? That's not fair (4)

7 Ladies: what one does there, having first taken off clothes (9)

8 Bad steer, to incite one who may go out on a limb (4,7)

12 Second-hand story of papal toe? (5,6)

14 Fiery spirit of monk bringing round power tool (10)

16 After-dinner speaker perhaps disturbs our trance (9)

20 Become endlessly stupid, and like horror stories (6)

23 There you are in France, picking up one instrument (5)

24 Member with independent opinion (4)

27 Star students on the way up (3)

Solution see page 258

ACROSS

1 Brie melted in air? That's serious (8)

5 Papers returned with date inserted in agreement (2,4)

9 Drama not composed willy–nilly (2,6)

10 Outside link accommodating short study (6)

11 Apparently true conservative Republican can be taken in (8)

12 Think about returning wine present (6)

14 Encourage cook, perhaps, to provide snack (3,2,5)

18 It requires perfect vision to get this score on board (6,4)

22 Two flats? That sounds rich (6)

23 With constant coverage, novel can't get contract (8)

24 Extremely ticklish open garments made of leather? (6)

25 Independent small spacecraft, one based in Sicily? (8)

26 Second-hand vehicles lacking leads had to be carried (6)

27 Place trap underground with modern technology (8)

DOWN

1 Charges about having lost good rifle (6)

2 Called out plot to capture animal shelter (6)

3 Note on black French artist (6)

4 English not crazy for flashy displays (4,6)

6 Outstanding former PM is straight up (3,5)

7 Quickly pass on insult (4,4)

8 Bring down average speed (8)

13 City replaces masthead in general correspondence (10)

15 Record second thoughts about recent requirement for country reps (2,6)

16 Philosopher irritated when declared to be like everyone else (8)

17 Whole green bananas can cause a bad reaction (8)

19 Food for new recruits (6)

20 Get to chaps minding tot (6)

21 Deplore being endlessly cruel (6)

Solution see page 258

ACROSS

9 Wildfowlers besiege a French plant (9)

10 Heron, say, on top of tree (5)

11 One cold diver turns over chunk of glacier (7)

12 Feature in garden party with superb sandwiches (7)

13 Whitish yellow growth that climbs walls (5)

14 Plant English or Greek character in plot (3,6)

16 TV documentary strand animating a rather dull town (3,7,5)

19 A Dubliner's about to take in dress for tiny bodies (9)

21 Briefly recognise lakes and hillock (5)

22 Problem in 8 for possibly blocking sound of 25? (4,3)

23 Crow unknown yacht that's docked in Douglas? (4,3)

24 Hard woman rejected cosmetic (5)

25 It flies Times into oil well at sea (6,3)

DOWN

1 Wasp I distracted circling plant (10)

2 They progress in leaps and bounds before eating cane up (8)

3 Small miner strips vertical end of quarry (6)

4 Grasp front of tartan rug (4)

5 What ass does to curb lazy women's rides (10)

6 How to shelter border road initially? This'll do it (8)

7 Clasp ring found in ancient tower (6)

8 Union probing phone system's boss (4)

14 Fly low with daring (10)

15 Vet books inspired by excited toddler (2,8)

17 A Greek heretic dealing with land (8)

18 Councillor's wearing jumper and vest for Swedes, maybe (4,4)

20 Nuts like tackling digital problem (6)

21 Stimulate class left without paper (6)

22 Ditch one hectare after another (2-2)

23 Flyer's second article abridged (4)

Solution see page 259

Clues are in alphabetical order of their solutions, which should be fitted in the grid jigsaw-wise, however they will go.

A Sugar refiner after fine salt (7)

B Brief horrors finding one trapped by move alongside runners (6,9)

C Metal put out, not uranium, for piece of armour (6)

D Could French author have ignored article there? (7)

E Line beneath edge cut for girdle (8)

F With a civil organisation coming under fire initially, steps taken in Madrid? (8)

G Somewhat like the country singer, he improvised (8)

H Body parts smell: spleen served up (6)

I A little money certain to improve Simpson by the law itself (4,4)

J Wild and psychoanalytical? (6)

K Horny teenager possibly getting to grips with love (8)

L On reflection, nothing is in corporation for polyglot (8)

M Tory passing between two holiday islands, the first timeless, noted montage? (7,8)

N Deny entrance from the southwest? (6)

O People left, those remaining originally abandoned (6)

P Plant wolf destroyed — animal trained? (7)

Q Pretty dresses still for Spanish royalist (8)

R Primate in error, he's useless (6)

S Second four axes maintaining good alignment, scientifically (6)

T Law enforcers into justice that's poetic (8)

U Bowl underarm, rolling it nearly as low for openers (6)

V Bert madly embraced by girl supporter (8)

W Wifelet enjoyed mud bath (8)

X Chinese-named region ultimately making fascist areas after uprising (6)

Y God found by old solvers in religious school (7)

Z Cross river, though only second half critical (6)

Solution see page 259

ACROSS

9 Fish and fruit wonderful in Spain (5,4)

10 To be mad not having succeeded is foolish (5)

11 Printing house that is making a gift (7)

12 Become fine again? Explain (5,2)

13 A team of detectives is sharp (4)

14 Favouring English athlete: one came first (10)

15 Extremist Rees-Mogg elected (7)

17 Capri: so awfully dull (7)

19 Free, so vacation in province (4,6)

22 One may be bent back, needing to be shortened (4)

23 Hung about with protective coat, I can enter (7)

24 Young lady repelling favourite put foot in it? (7)

26 Lunge not working? Not quite all (5)

27 One attacking a holy book in speech (9)

DOWN

1 Joint camp launch in chaos, so many changes to be made here (7,8)

2 Liable to forget one's problem (8)

3 Soldiers, perhaps: GI avoids huge types (4)

4 Reduce intensity? No we don't, unfortunately (4,4)

5 After short pause, signal recovery (6)

6 Musical direction we hear written out badly (8)

7 Said noble is without hope of heir (6)

8 People in SUVs? Ones like Virginia — heavens! (7,8)

16 Be outside a quiet prison (8)

17 Most prudish minister receiving medal (8)

18 Mark up article not consumed (8)

20 Check the fiery inmate (6)

21 Athletic team's out-of-date meat (6)

25 Whisky cocktail perhaps disagreeable (4)

Solution see page 259

34 Set by Nutmeg

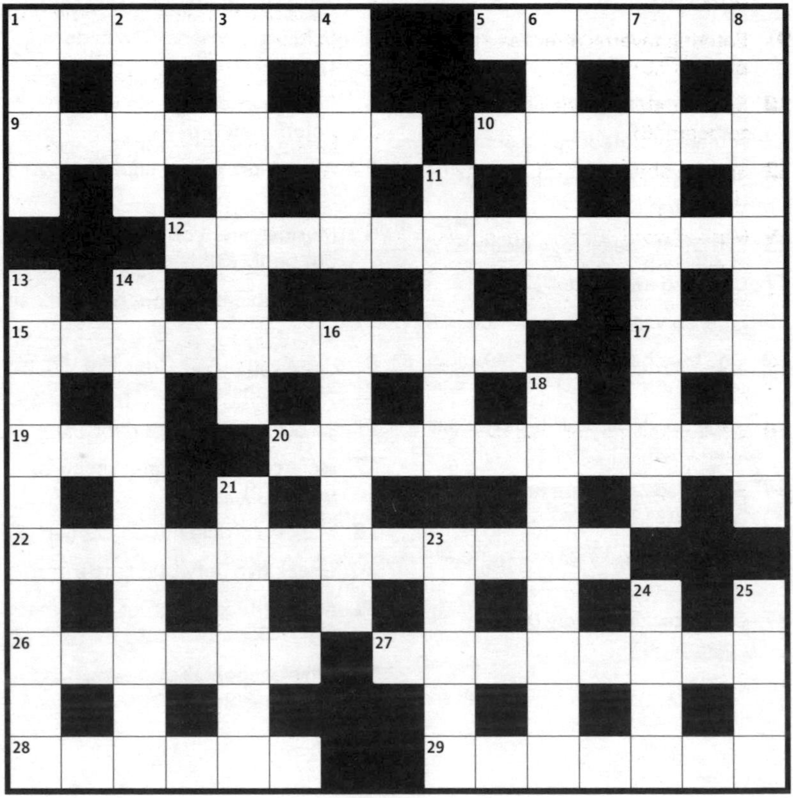

ACROSS

1 Cockney hunted down on policeman's first beat (7)

5 Many trousers briefly removed (4,2)

9 Entering taverns after tea, I'll be bound (2,6)

10 Singular athlete, one accustomed to beam (6)

12 Spaces aboard for officers' suits? (12)

15 Marked word such as we initially check with editor (10)

17 Yankee cracking clue oddly rejected solution (3)

19 Aquatic mammal seabird caught (3)

20 Where deal may be had by mad ruler on the move? (10)

22 Emotive outcome of corruption at police HQ? (12)

26 Portiolo quietly splitting gave the game away (6)

27 Number of customers in time to pay for trip (8)

28 Plodded into the Home Counties and moved on apace (6)

29 Immature swimmer bit staff (7)

DOWN

1 Puritan outfit under pressure (4)

2 Remarkable Scots centre missed by world heritage guardians (4)

3 Make use of frame one trimmed (4,4)

4 Duke, working men's benefactor (5)

6 First man from south to join a king's fleet (6)

7 Preserve place for wine dispenser at table (4,6)

8 Where crops may be grown after dams burst close to Paris? (10)

11 Tenor's last note upset acoustic device (6)

13 Sailors attending course find something to keep them going (5,5)

14 Possible source of firing put poacher off (10)

16 Nothing titillating? Not quite (6)

18 Gunners turning up refreshed, ran in (8)

21 Poet's 'void land south of river' (6)

23 Sleep with sailor in bunk? (5)

24 Served up duck with potato dressing (4)

25 Last of pickers still to grade fruit (4)

Solution see page 260

ACROSS

7 Compromising exchanges foolishly flirting Fancy–Fancy at first dares to produce (5-4)

8 Mind sheikhdom deporting a husband (5)

9 Tried playing record earlier? Rubbish! (9)

10 Spy No 2 in Slovakia (5)

12 Moon, showing bum in front of polite society (6)

13 Varied the City football team, after first half's reversal (8)

16 Working near the capital (7)

19 Sexy garments making comeback in popular nightclub? (7)

22 Recognises clue about breaks for refuelling (3,5)

25 Greek character amongst posters becoming pests (6)

27 Bowler in match between close rivals (5)

28 Places for burying 15s around a fellow doctor (9)

29 What most 15s have — dogs, too! (5)

30 Structure of cell makes criminal groan at lifestyle mag (9)

DOWN

1 Rage consuming one 10 (6)

2 Bad clue butchered by editor originally (can be trained) (8)

3 Architect agreed with son (6)

4 No longer pending? Right, get busy! (7)

5 Theme involves recipe for a certain degree of latitude? (6)

6 Roman summer resort of note (first book in series) (6)

11 Fashion leaders in Ascot outfits look stunning too (4)

14, 15 Cartoon series, a much cooler version of 16 17? (3,3)

16, 17 Broken hot tap? Best cover item in film (3,3)

18 Very small bit of a 15? (4)

20 Small child's train? Half of it has defaced LNER glass (8)

21 A step taken by theme's essential character to become a film star (7)

23 Superhero gets cinema rocking (6)

24 Refined what some tenants may do when rent finally gets raised (6)

25 Icon sporting a cravat? Not initially (6)

26 Gardener's tool having removed what's on 14, OK to eat outside of beetroot? (6)

Solution see page 260

Set by Matilda

ACROSS

1 Universal start of sale promotion for Marvel productions? (6)

5 Disadvantage of ward (8)

9 Spin monster's 'going forward' (8)

10 Magicians missing trick? There are a dozen in a box (6)

11 Friendly bug maybe regularly found in fruit (12)

13,22 Hot stuff is awfully ripe — you can say that again! (4-4)

14 Like fillet? Be grateful for eating one (8)

17 Portray one patient for cosmetic treatment (5,3)

18 Void and somewhat illunderstood rejection (4)

20 Appearing before the Guardian's motley crew: a lot are no oil paintings! (12)

23 Cycling mostly with Matilda in minimal attire (6)

24 Put at risk X after heart transplant (8)

25 Suckling a French ewe and failing (8)

26 Little backing of one busy in intelligence (3,3)

DOWN

2 Tips of oversized and really sharp blades (4)

3 Fighter helping movement of the people (9)

4 Tweets leading to crazy speech (6)

5 BBC sold out media broadcast at a loss (15)

6 Next, a record player? That needs a bit of money (8)

7 Polish up on question and answer — definitely not a 23! (5)

8 In slapdash manner around Gravesend without wheels (10)

12 Fed up in the morning, Anto is upset about one slur (10)

15 Scene of promontory by the outskirts of Lagos (9)

16 Even Johnson's initially working out notice for expulsion (8)

19 Line from fox or rabbit argument (6)

21 Best of the pre-Raphaelites (5)

22 See 13

Solution see page 260

37 Set by Picaroon

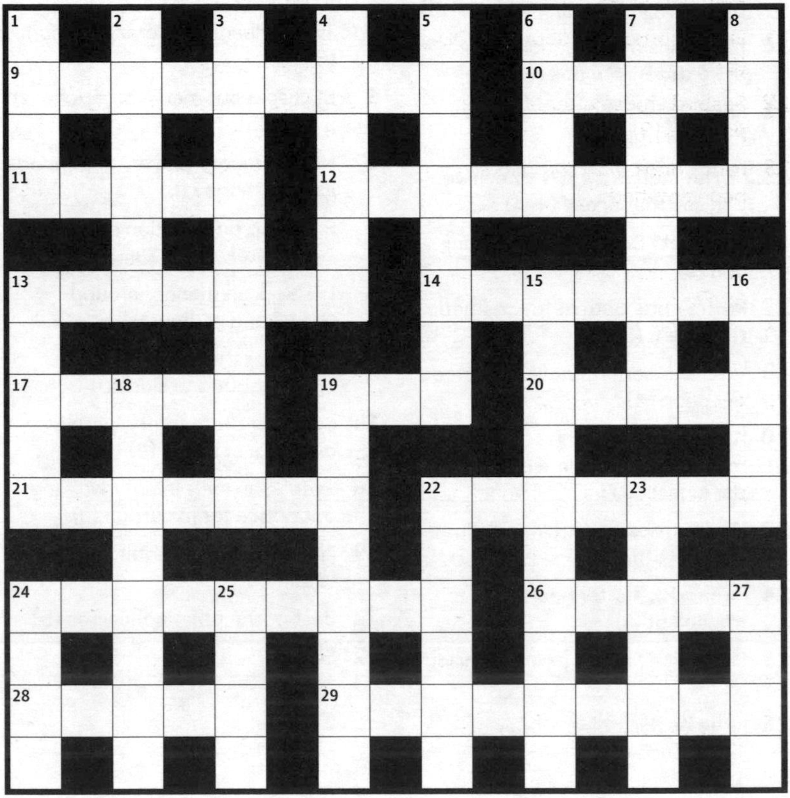

ACROSS

9 Are they still development areas? (9)

10 Inspiring figure to speak after switching sides (5)

11 Fierce sort of row about £1,000 (5)

12 Seabird I rouse after Manx cat, perhaps (9)

13 Fancy drink, with sherry having been emptied (7)

14 See 22

17 Vehicle must follow very old terms (5)

19 Like some wines, this doesn't last long! (3)

20 Alcohol in Asia contains new twist (5)

21 Male's small jumper with shortened back (7)

22,14 Event now associated with elements of 10, 24, 28, 29, 3, 4, 8,

23 and four other solutions (7,3,4)

24 Leather dancing shoe hired (9)

26 Spirit said to show spirit (5)

28 Daisy's back into phoney exoticism (5)

29 Attack, as a farmer may (4,1,2,2)

DOWN

1 Raised energy in regime change (4)

2 Put on wrapping paper, which is to prove tedious (4,2)

3 Trickster's gossip in support of British ruler (4,6)

4,27 King's tucked into bread loaves or snacks (6,4)

5 I really drink and like some drinks (8)

6 Shop one managed to put up (4)

7 Cuban steps in stadium with sound of contempt rising (8)

8 Big cheese from Italy to follow starter of eggs (4)

13 Frenzy? Not so many, when halfhearted? (5)

15 Islander is wanted in training (4,6)

16 Judge once concerned with one found guilty of stealing fruit (5)

18 Executives with love for a vocal group (8)

19 Channel for auditor having got rid of The Kinks (8)

22 Corps given permission to split up (6)

23 Electronic stuff working for imitator (6)

24 Circle dance goes around in a circle (4)

25 It's used to fence bounds of estate hosting games (4)

27 See 4

Solution see page 261

Set by Philistine

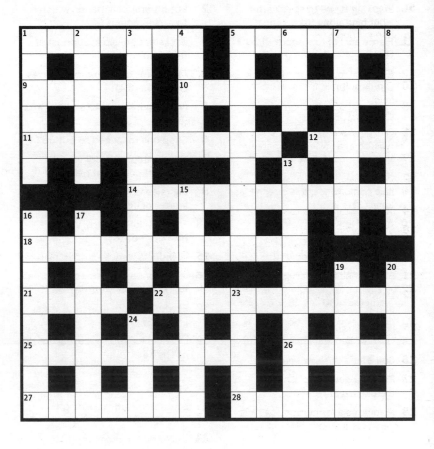

ACROSS

1 Lancer told to choose an entrance (7)

5 Went down as a result of what happened in a gastric haemorrhage (7)

9 House sold off around mid–April (5)

10 City is suitable for everyone involved in commercial vehicle insurance (9)

11 Girl, nine, starts wearing ponytail twisted in an affecting manner (10)

12 Writer having a change of heart and spirit (4)

14 That guy talks to turbans? (11)

18 Staff working to prop organisation, but not too much (2,3,6)

21 Bloody half of literary device (4)

22 Deceptive advocacy of dire perils and sin (2,7)

25 Leaving us can make it relax and wallow (9)

26 See 6

27 Route to get 'bravo' out of theatre land (7)

28 Medium or perhaps strong? You can have instant coffee at first (7)

DOWN

1 Agent cut up for bowel problem (6)

2 Magpie? Five to feature in my papers (6)

3 Dines out with song to provide some realism (10)

4 2 given intravenously (5)

5 Like Bob Dylan in blue and brown, heartlessly plugged out (7,2)

6,26 New motion, top item to be debated (4,5)

7 Oliver is having one portion? Must be feeling queasy (8)

8 One little and quiet place to sleep on the river (8)

13 Me, 21, grappling with a PhD in population studies (10)

15 One on the tail of pair planning lurid hijacking (3,6)

16 Criminal unclothed to reveal somebody with no special powers (8)

17 Refusing food when a refusal reportedly damages you (8)

19 Complete and utter European (6)

20 Digestive movement with vigour (6)

23 Expensive soak in marinade (5)

24 2 involved in murder (4)

Solution see page 261

ACROSS

7 Emperor in cape others in Rome drag back inside (8)

9 Like some remedies brother turned over, central to cure (6)

10 Cheese having fine character from its source (4)

11 Repeat mistake of first woman in public television (4,3,3)

12 As starter for lunch, tucked into game at table (6)

14 Nothing right about fake news? That's more than fair (8)

15 What's good in dish with pastry covering? (6)

17 Place in Europe British bunglers oddly forfeited (6)

20 Method learnt differently in North American city (8)

22 Get in boat at sea (6)

23 Impression about article by journalists being downer (10)

24 Person writing second message shortened by 60% (4)

25 Look — openers in batting order seen in pavilion (6)

26 Peers enjoy it — also English upper classes once (8)

DOWN

1 Attachment from down under going astray in the mail, PS left out (8)

2 Family internally raised capital (4)

3 Become exhausted, so bring about dismissal (3,3)

4 Second US president, across time, was highly inaccurate in pursuing goal (4,4)

5 Inexperienced and unimportant? Okay (5,5)

6 Beginning completed over a year (3,3)

8 Energy put into singular achievement in games — like the Olympics (3-3)

13 Settle on location for putting lime, say (5,5)

16 75% of display in public was excessive (8)

18 Sailor using his head in final art on board (8)

19 Hundreds initially fleeing icy enclosure in autumn, so to speak (3,3)

21 At unspecified time, not enough to raise capital? (3,3)

22 Escape from disastrous tour with global organisation (6)

24 So leaves person from one African country for another (4)

Solution see page 261

In celebration of a centenary

ACROSS

7 VIPs training in it hurtle around circuit the wrong way! (6-3)

8 Policeman's a poser in pictures (5)

9 Bridge declaration — going first is one for the old grey cells (9)

10 24 makes a journey in the interior (5)

12 Old rebel who initiates drugs bust in a hospital? (6)

13 24 nurse faces demand from those wanting answers (8)

16 24 ending early: transport put on (7)

19 Rubbing noses abroad, missionaries converted 24 (7)

22 Trade centre stocking some knocked–off 24 (8)

25 Perhaps Bruce doubles as 6's relative (6)

27 She hunted, and I shot a 21 (5)

28 He's really missed the combination of today's themes (9)

29 In what's written, crossword setter's reduced complicated devices (5)

30 Topless rockers opening pipe get punchy with cryptic contrivance (6,3)

DOWN

1 Outlaw receives word that may surprise 24 (6)

2 24 compilers will dress with jumper (8)

3 Hunt for words in grid? Perhaps reading in, start to see every one (6)

4 24's more sluggish son preferred to daughter (7)

5 Pelmanism tests this area where people play everything (6)

6 Taking flight from here to America, about to tackle a grid-filling problem (6)

11 Passage taken by Greeks to Agora — or from letters to 28 (4)

14 Might they be used regularly in Ulmeni? (3)

15 24 is zati? You shouldn't take the odds … (3)

16 … where to see punter's tips for Chepstow and Musselburgh? (3)

17 Short fat god (3)

18 Mummy bear pours away just a bit (4)

20 Engineer maybe suppressing an opening for grease 24 (8)

21 It's found between breasts and rear ends when one goes topless (7)

23 Number one is obsessive about, say … (6)

24 … mass being sung at the correct pitch (6)

25 Awkward jump while skating in Kentucky (6)

26 'Predated' now 'pronated' because of this boffin (6)

Solution see page 262

41 Set by Paul

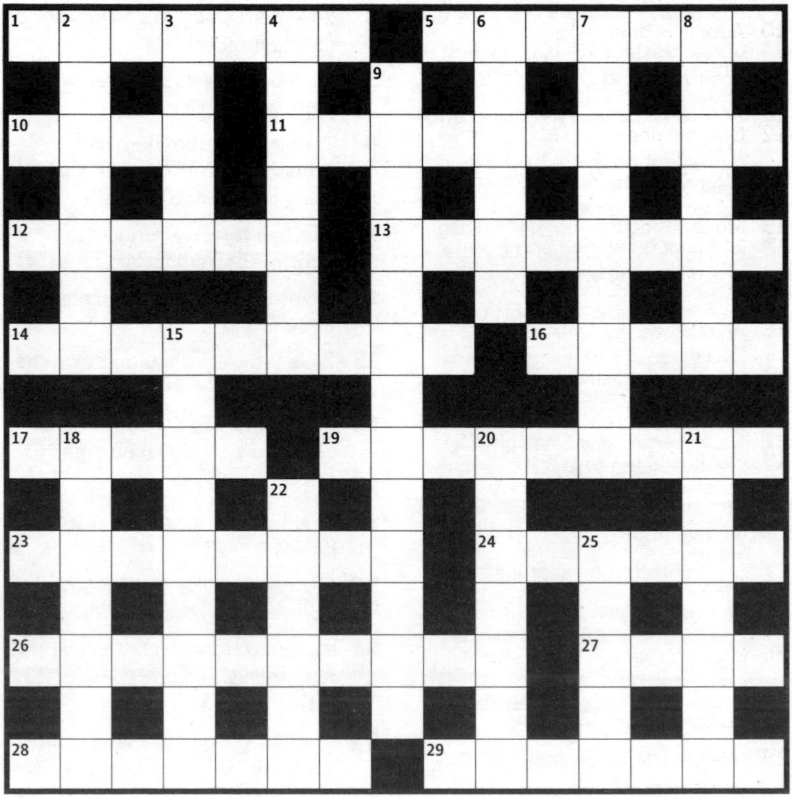

ACROSS

1 Call from the US electorate? (2-5)

5 Mysterious flash enveloping trailer (7)

10 Adonis is boss (4)

11 Retro plain squares under the table, perhaps? (2,3,5)

12 God placing 6 and Egyptian equivalent back-to-back behind you (6)

13 More difficult check reviewed on god (8)

14 Female god performs (4,1,4)

16 Worshipper for whom church in Dudley providing sanctuary (5)

17 Half-Vulcan box contains head of Prometheus (5)

19 Hard work initially, easier otherwise to maintain order (9)

23 Wonderful goddess hiding in wood (4-4)

24 Goddess concealing second of beauty spots (6)

26 Chaotic form disowned, happy to come first (6,4)

27 Reach god by bus, finally (4)

28 'We have arrived', daughter announced (7)

29 Most immediate gain overwhelming god (7)

DOWN

2 North American province, not a different South American city (7)

3 Artist's country escaping Roman god (5)

4 When heavenly body drops idle god (7)

6 God dressing priest in short stockings (6)

7 Island originally home to climbing marsupial — one of these is as dead as a dodo? (9)

8 Mass inspiring god, Mars' device? (7)

9 Where Morpheus might live to dream, more bunks emptied out (6,7)

15 Close game receives outstanding support, finally (9)

18 God lifting couple into drink (7)

20 Nemesis rising, for example, over my dead body (7)

21 Heaven-bound American uncle entertaining European women inspired by Dionysus (7)

22 Goddess putting second and third of 21 in order? (6)

25 I won't ever remove lid from inverted can! (2,3)

Solution see page 262

42

Set by Vlad

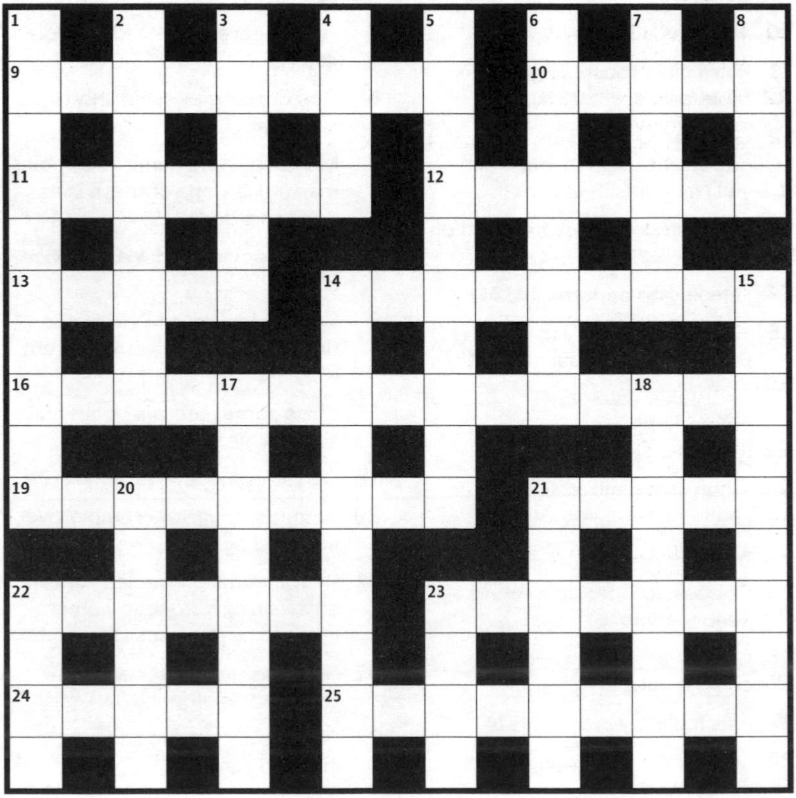

ACROSS

9 Wake father — am getting worried about time (9)

10 Ginger gets glasses at the going rate (5)

11 Rejection of Thatcher that is unlimited (4,3)

12 Thanks to exercise, looking hot and sweaty but gradually got thinner (7)

13 Ruling country's in talks (5)

14 Under restriction — swine keeps on vilifying leaders (5,4)

16 Read nothing — that, he felt, could be Trump's area of expertise? (3,3,2,3,4)

19 Allen at the start breaks cue and rest (9)

21 Wine bar stocks old (5)

22 Conference venue spitting feathers — bar knocked back (7)

23 Grumble incessantly about watch (7)

24 Beg editor to withdraw material (5)

25 Neared solution after official votes (9)

DOWN

1 Do no more about problems raised by Queen (4,6)

2 'Time that was gone', as the middle dropped out (5,3)

3 Show signs of annoyance in bedroom — useless? (6)

4 Book by president is dear (4)

5 Photograph club athlete (4-6)

6 Mate finally scored during match (8)

7 Unprepared stuff the writer's both for and against (6)

8 Told off, Charlie kept out of sight (4)

14 Drink? Rare politician maintains resistance (6,4)

15 Containing infection initially difficult for leader — this way's less hassle (6,4)

17 Present-day worker drops precious recording (8)

18 Tough no longer playing (8)

20 Count carrying more weight after transitioning (6)

21 Start to straighten sheets for escort, as a gentleman does (6)

22 Heard about US writer's affectation (4)

23 Strike during scuffle (4)

Solution see page 262

Set by Brummie

ACROSS

8 Laid up in old island state (8)

9 Could be a barnacle's inappropriate prod (5)

10 Stupid person cutting end off sun-dried meat strips (4)

11 Scandalous secrets revealed to chambermaid (5,5)

12 Robin playing over intro of boy band (6)

14 Agent who changes players going round country with no capital (8)

16 A despicable person gets put away in stir (7)

18 The City Beautiful's light surrounded by gold ring (7)

21 Oddball sailor working over marines by a lake (8)

23 Royal broadcast copies (6)

24 Seabed and bank rocks that produce wind? (5,5)

26, 2 Trips in central Kurdistan initially become unhealthy (4,4)

27 Area of Northumberland that's handy for suckers? (5)

28 Master knight called Hill (8)

DOWN

1 Scales tipped against popular government leader taking a rest (8)

2 See 26 across

3 Mean to follow this middle course (6)

4 No flyer needs oxygen, by the way — laughable! (7)

5 Like certain sisters said 'fruit' (4)

6 Short time I'd arranged with ailing artist (10)

7 Corner the rest of Members of Parliament (6)

13 Uncommunicative book put out — end is awful (8,2)

15 Salt content of tobacco (3)

17 Bell's unfinished book (3)

19 Avoid fish and small fowl (8)

20 Canned eels can have a purifying effect (7)

22 Cracker from a tube, possibly today's last (6)

23 Danish father's go? (6)

25 Honey bishop hid in tree (4)

26 Bow adjuster changed for good (4)

Solution see page 263

ACROSS

7 10001000 teachers might be kind of shy (7)

8 Labour employs leading economist over article for growth (7)

9 Small child's slide? (4)

10 Old church's financial backers lose pound sterling in trades (9)

12 Break back carrying wife's deposits as security (5)

13 They send out Mister Messy to collect note (8)

15 In the end policies bore, admit focus groups (4)

16 Partners suppress anger with alarm (5)

17 Remove stolen contents (4)

18 Plant has Ubers manufactured (3,5)

20 Perhaps Shakespeare eats no more (6)

21 Kept, as are exotic birds (9)

22 Cricket, maybe, is mega-excited (4)

24 Gap garment a third off — over nine grand! (7)

25 Something unusual in books about lovesick Yankee (7)

DOWN

1 Men bowled over by fine bird ... (4)

2 ... and more court daughter with slow dancing (4,4)

3 College in Cambridge or in New York? (6)

4 Number it: a 100 written up as symbols (8)

5 Champion in utter darkness (6)

6 Nails cut up (4)

11 Former party leader inherits real mess and can be excused (9)

12 A little bit of quiet on the radio (5)

14 Even reversing, I would be quick (5)

16 It's beautiful out (8)

17 Arguments with scientists about fish (8)

19 Hit golf ball badly over river, then withdrawn (7)

20 Holy man to dance around his building (6)

21 Dads drink on Sunday (4)

23 Worried to support married couple (4)

Solution see page 263

ACROSS

9 Change after a boxing match, as soldiers may be ordered (5,4)

10 Give one's view, nothing long (5)

11 Travel protected by explosive weapon (7)

12 With words of acceptance, married: later so alone (7)

13 Needing exercise, one circles a furlong (5)

14 Control working and income (9)

16 Gun shop price war may show value of money (10,5)

19 Prepare war orders for Flying Squad (3,6)

21 Wait to eat a Malaysian dish (5)

22 Went for a drive; may it have been clocked? (4,3)

23 Explosion, after which children all fall down? (7)

24 English in clothes for stylish people (5)

25 One in a rush to claim riches involved demon girl (4,5)

DOWN

1 Wall painting survives, higher (4,6)

2 Work of editor extremely desirable (2,3,3)

3 Relaxing in an exam covering one of the three basics? (2,4)

4 Leave, almost completely (4)

5 Conflicted, paired off to maintain attention (2,3,5)

6 Sudden chill: mild illnesses need sleep (4,4)

7 Two bottles unfinished? This situation benefits us both (3–3)

8 Woman's meeting daughter in crowd (4)

14 Record how old we are to dampen enthusiasm (10)

15 Road sorely in need of repair sooner than usual (5,5)

17 Awkward person playing charades (4,4)

18 Sort of brief observation (8)

20 Is very nervous of locks (6)

21 Opening foreign letter with edge of thumb makes bad mark (6)

22 Tongue's fur due for scraping (4)

23 In the car, I take the wheel (4)

Solution see page 263

46 Set by Matilda

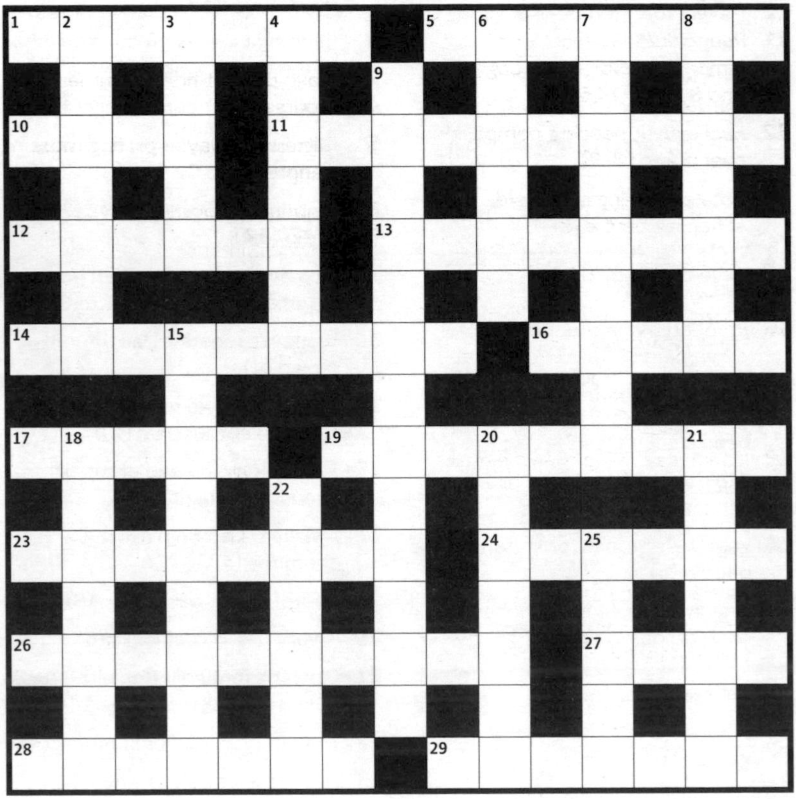

ACROSS

1,5 Late professor's nephew as knight errant (7,7)

10 Shock as tabloid pinches Telegraph leader (4)

11 Patsy forced to fast? Finishes off Limoncello, Cointreau, cognac and Scotch (1,4,5)

12 Feel empty, needing compassion over dump (3-3)

13 Irritated seeing rat outside shopping centre (8)

14 Not seeing straight when angry, I'd say (5-4)

16 Emotion not in order for this movement (2,3)

17 Criminal humanoid turned fine (5)

19 Insect, say, flying over the moon (2,7)

23 Tintin's struggling with Haddock's sixth sense (8)

24 Rue de Pierre Gretzky (6)

26 Very well, dish out punishment covered by brief (2,4,4)

27 Savage flower (4)

28 It hurts to wear jewellery in this game (7)

29 Note about covering musicians (7)

DOWN

2 Honorary Tory leader implicated in kinky ritual (7)

3 Point out a winemaker (5)

4 Illustration no longer sufficient? (7)

6 Last, but not first, swimmer is off course (6)

7 Kittens to play — getting most tangled (9)

8 Impossible bottle party? (2,3,2)

9 At first, cinemagoer natters rudely during tear-jerker, causing dismay (13)

15 Initially terrified, Warhol is being treated for poor hearing (4,5)

18 Encounter with Mac could become unromantic (3,4)

20 Sweet is almost entirely à la crème pudding (7)

21 Thief working separately without nav (7)

22 Junior doctor for Bury and Wigan at last (6)

25 Ditch solving Sudoku — all real silly in the end (5)

Solution see page 264

Set by Nutmeg

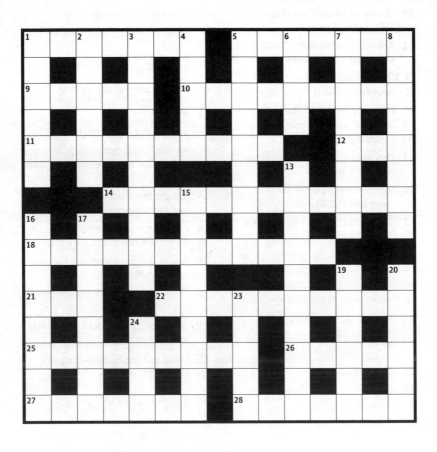

ACROSS

1 Shady location for surfers (4,3)

5 Heretical movement beyond control after number retired (7)

9 Turn, facing celebrity's back (5)

10 Muslim land in east joining assembly of UN at last (9)

11,12 Abridged song a source of inspiration (10,3)

14 Formerly arm 25% of workforce? (12)

18 On the verge of binding the enemy over — it's taken long enough! (5,4,3)

21,22 Nationals from banks of Nile roam south, full of enthusiasm (3,10)

25 Damaged elastic wears thin (2,3,4)

26 Italian team's season not begun (5)

27 Better in French clubs avoiding risk (7)

28 Proxy rule regarding unopened office (7)

DOWN

1 Dramatist on vacation taking in legendary show (6)

2 Do up bows of each vessel within slipway (6)

3 First of items dropped by steward behind small storage containers (5,5)

4 Footing bill, initially lacking change (5)

5 Peruse underlying facts about primitive duck (9)

6 Old ladies switched venue for sporting event (4)

7 Delinquent, one that's sadly dropped out (8)

8 Leave fair, out of sorts (5,3)

13 Phenomenal cockney pooch caught in a police trap (10)

15 Repeat fee European bank first set up (9)

16 Mum queueing where traffic's heaviest? (4,4)

17 Plague hunter possibly gets two-hour shift (3,5)

19 Bell-ringer's relations not converted (6)

20 Raptor thus brought up its food (6)

23 Nearer snatching the lead, but never a victor (5)

24 Unrewarding tip (4)

Solution see page 264

ACROSS

9 Putting on this jumper, male player might relax here (5,4)

10 Mark part of bible to introduce round church (5)

11 Boozer to call jerk this? (7)

12 Respecting wedding party (7)

13 On the house that's detached (4)

14 Detailed notice beside posters and flyers (10)

15 Book store (7)

17 Shepherd and sheep going over sedimentary rock, mostly (7)

19 Everyday performer, having a lot of fresh sprouts (sign of Christmas)? (5,5)

22 Tip off a Romeo to get into woman's skirt (4)

23 Muscle work out is clear (7)

24 Break up gang fight behind clubs (7)

26 Supporters gathering around the last for Tiger Woods (5)

27 Instruct nurses to cover daytime (9)

DOWN

1 After you season in preparation for dish (3,6,6)

2 Start of lesson, they bring in students (8)

3 After playing both sides of cassette (4)

4 Cave in woody area: everyone enters the wrong way (8)

5 All clothing for baby one mother prepared for unborn child (6)

6 Hamper with food additive to eat cold (8)

7 As one chooses a checkout with divides (2,4)

8 Set off in clearness, then they go up in flames (7,8)

16 Do solitary? Her Majesty's pleasure for this one? (8)

17 Mark cryptic clue for tiny thing (8)

18 Nut loaf remnant (8)

20 Shared out presents he helps to deliver? (6)

21 Plants kiss on middle of cheek: love comes first, absolutely (2-4)

25 Press to take one game for review (4)

Solution see page 264

49

Set by Picaroon

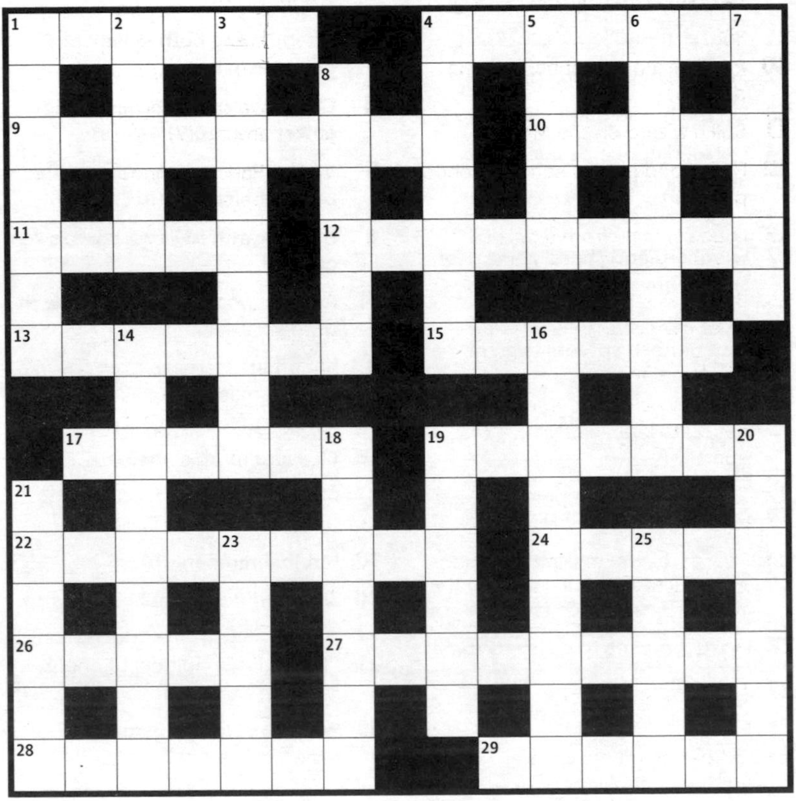

ACROSS

1,4 Slogan here shows big heart protecting society (6,7)

9 Content to leave demure aunt terribly flushed, getting changed (9)

10 Puzzle from personnel wearing drag (5)

11 Still a wizard on the Mac? (5)

12 Hollywood actor's name in school plays (9)

13 Loose shingle from a part of these shores (7)

15 Bobby who managed, 28 after what thief does (6)

17 See 8

19 Wrongly call this person strict, not quite keeping two metres apart (7)

22 Two six-footers importing regular doses of insulin for payee (9)

24 Pour in dry white wine, not a mild, as and when (2,3)

26 Feature framing ring and choker (5)

27 The people I survey in Ohio getting shocked (3,6)

28,29 Seeking office, British PM loses European conflict (7,6)

DOWN

1,21 Plot made to work, nurtured by criminal's patient approach? (7,6)

2 Natasha's heart stolen by guy's divine gift (5)

3 Kiss in film, touching film, one going all the way (9)

4 Casanova slims down, turning jacket around (7)

5 Where Paris was once, without end or beginning (5)

6 By the way, you'll find one broken and set out (9)

7,20 European runner collects outstanding coat this makes fit (6,7)

8, 17 Cher may open this, which prevents issue (6,6)

14 Like sprouts and maize, hot not cold, for a starter (9)

16 A star led by stud in dance (5,4)

18 He speeds round in awfully hard turn northward (7)

19 Crossword setter's not quite stupid or fabulous (6)

20 See 7

21 See 1

23 British rebels rising up in Argentine city (5)

25 Slave man, one found in auction (5)

Solution see page 265

50

Set by Paul

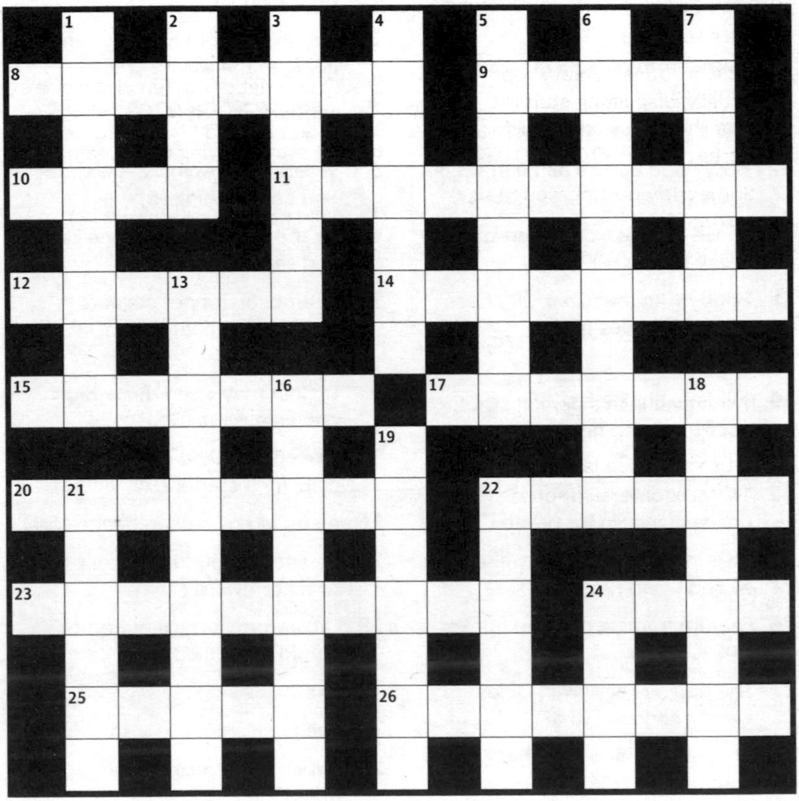

ACROSS

8 Tilt when boarding does for vessel (8)

9 10's first cut where 25 kept (5)

10,25 Plane, for example, common flyer stripped? (9)

11,3,2 Consuming chewy rope initially, disgusting stuff like that they say is unlawful for performers at 10 25? (10,0,6,4)

12 Somebody putting wedge back on rug (6)

14 Private sector that is failing (8)

15 See 24 down

17 Female doctor I kiss, performer at 10 25 (7)

20 Builder's drink, particular taste (3,2,3)

22 Yet to embrace fashion, performers at 10 25 (3,3)

23 A git loading safe weapon for kids (10)

24 Bloody exceptional (4)

25 See 10

26 Presumably odd time for anticlimax (3–5)

DOWN

1 Guzzle tasty sandwiches second (8)

2 See 11

3 See 11

4 Peach biscuit (7)

5 10 25 relations in female dance finished, almost (4,4)

6 Hit often proving fatal, seeing died, possibly? (6,4)

7 Cold heart of oil burner? (6)

13 Bound to support Gates's baby, just look at what's in store! (6–4)

16 Designs right number of masts on brig, for example, carried by ships (8)

18 Natural gas in neither fluid (8)

19 Temperature inside loco that hasn't started rising for performers at 10 25 (7)

21 Tense difficult, might you say? (6)

22 County cricket side in Mediterranean city (6)

24,15 Performer at 10 25 of what a Turk might do to enthral his capital, briefly? (4,7)

Solution see page 265

Set by Pan

ACROSS

1 Crafty animal getting last of food (6)

4 Optical illusion created by image moving over river (6)

9 Something used by students to study in bed (4)

10 Silly me! Heroin taken during voyages in military vessels once (5,5)

11 Cake that's special gone off (6)

12 Vocalist entertaining a Latin author (8)

13 Part of year depicted in end of sonnet by old poet (9)

15 Goddess heard in place to stable horses (4)

16 Course provided by alternative practitioner leaving base close to Oslo (4)

17 Last warning about women close to retirement getting money for the future (9)

21 Patent obtained by a patient's first carer? (8)

22 Attempt to keep one pound in hat (6)

24 Relative taking extremely tender stable hand to a safe place (10)

25 Source of chef's cooking fat causing wind (4)

26 Former partner playing tune in order to leave the stage (6)

27 One with obsessive interest in the origin of Arabia translated Koran (6)

DOWN

1 Fight about retro tool (7)

2 Bird runs over waste receptacle (5)

3 Twins wrong to take drugs to one appearing in court (7)

5 Naughty child meeting a large American animal (6)

6 Articles on European Union kept by fellow returning to old seat of learning (9)

7 Fast train meant primarily for Luxembourg's third head of state (7)

8 Unease caused by Conservative standing in for magnificent leader in enormous country (13)

14 Cops tricked individual supplying class A drug (9)

16 Tube for liquid in mine covering domestic source of electricity (7)

18 Tomato spilt on new silken fabric (7)

19 Toff beat old club on the golf course (7)

20 Former president of America consumed by misguided anger (6)

23 Experience cold during most of season (5)

Solution see page 265

52 Set by Pasquale

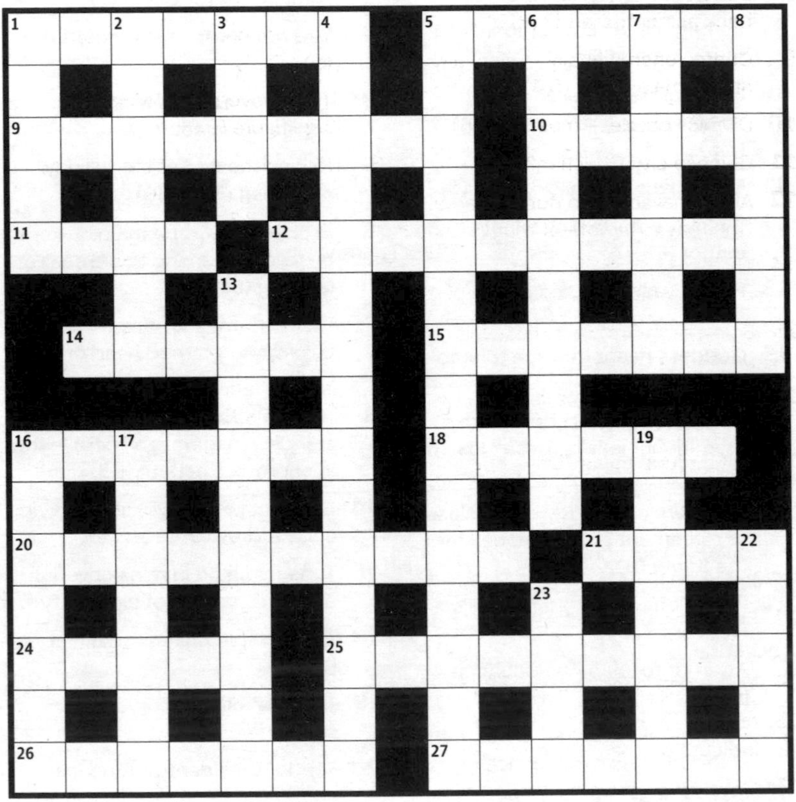

ACROSS

1 Very good Austen novel when keeping quiet in the afternoon (3,4)

5 Bad booze endlessly knocked back as contraband? (7)

9 Charge enemy finally — viciously attack male beast (5,4)

10 Dismiss puzzle — must pee (5)

11 Chinese city Christian? (4)

12 An animal sound in outdoor area? One may take note of that (4,6)

14 The woman's covering part of body — what is that part? (6)

15 Being germ-free, is almost passed for work (7)

16 Rodents 'orrible woman has in the open on island (7)

18 Get a round going? Drink not available, we hear (3,3)

20 In Christian Union teach odd shape — this convert is still learning (10)

21 Passes time in classical fashion (4)

24 One judge is far from happy (5)

25 Man bitten by dog? One may indicate disease (9)

26 Good student losing heart, one gathers (7)

27 Taught nothing revolutionary after expression of disapproval (7)

DOWN

1 Old boy restricted by disease — one gets lots of letters (2,3)

2 Devastation in small community with new leader (7)

3 PM once having a supernatural power? (4)

4 Thrown overboard, Magnus — huge figure (9,6)

5 Nearing the end of the holiday, everything else having gone wrong? (2,3,4,6)

6 Girl, a female always getting a nasty illness (5,5)

7 Wicked rogues pinching 500 dollars in Haiti (7)

8 Lake Superior has trees and American flowers (7)

13 Bird certain to fly around river and around end of forest (6,4)

16 Bowing as a group around church (7)

17 Make faster progress than unfashionable people (7)

19 Loud user of tongue in a flash (7)

22 Instrument with arrows pointing north (5)

23 Spirit abuse needs to be cut by half (4)

Solution see page 266

53 Set by Puck

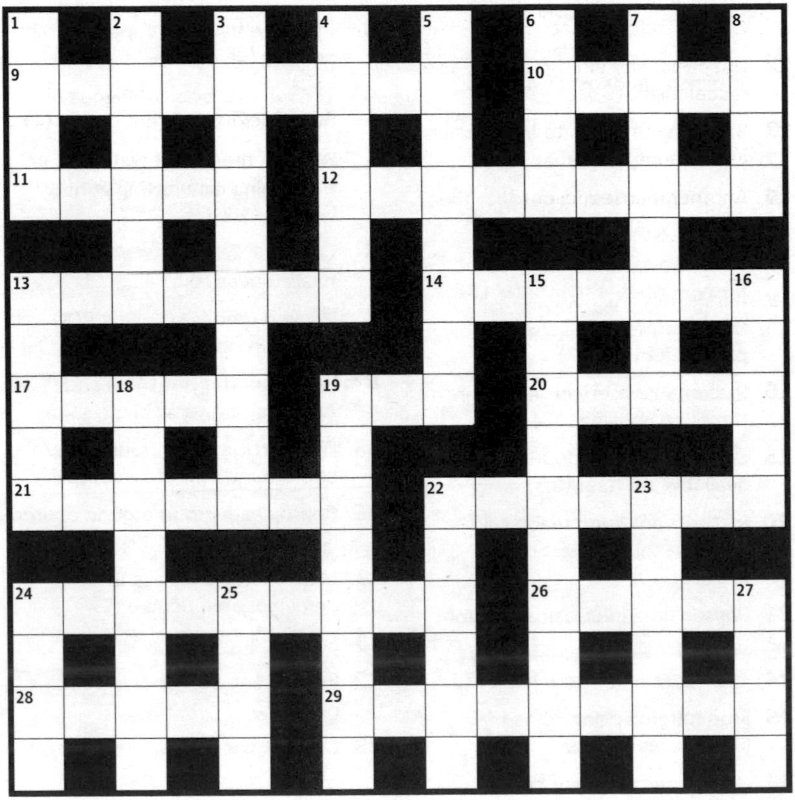

ACROSS

9 Papers can't lie? Wrong, just the same (9)

10 Is Puck good? Ring a friend (5)

11 Some 'iffy' remedies returned? On the surface, that's rough (5)

12 Upset our shy girl right away, as a rascal might (9)

13 Saw son cut down to 1, for easier assimilation (7)

14 Another married lover (7)

17 Game is second sale item not won (5)

19 Department investigating contracted detective's retirement (3)

20 Lots of actors originally starred in a musical (5)

21 Crack marksman departed with detective (7)

22 Name saint or pope? Brother no longer one (7)

24 Artist back in stock, in refined Colorado town (3,6)

26 Creamy-white, like a Welshman? (5)

28 Stoned female content to down 10 beers (5)

29 Playing darts, lady is mean and wicked! (9)

DOWN

1 See 24

2 Straight there, after travelling round (6)

3 Unadventurous guy? Then the woman stripped off (4-2-4)

4 Small-minded? Afraid so! (6)

5 Conservatives behind the Times newspaper, not the Scotsman (3,5)

6 Stood next to current queen (4)

7 Well-off area: right district selected originally for a Keith or Gordon? (8)

8 Doctor X, vegan animal rights activist (4)

13 Humming after crossword essentially well-constructed (5)

15 Flute? Part played is routine (10)

16 After tip-off, gets hold of fruit (5)

18 Farm vehicle turned up, worked into drawing (8)

19 Unfaithful lover is 4 after straying (8)

22 Death of European with no middle name (6)

23 Lots of people, 8 being the 25th of them? (6)

24,1 Long for the longer sleepers perhaps half of LNER and one third of LMS used (4-4)

25 Attention-seeking expression in article by the Edge (4)

27 More than one solver yet to finish? Child's play, perhaps, using this (2-2)

Solution see page 266

ACROSS

1 Drug dealer going after prison clerk (9)

6 See 22 down

8 Darling bursting at the seams almost? How elegant! (8)

9 Casual agreement to hold career back leads to destitution (6)

10 Elastic hem of bikini caught in bush? (6)

11 Juvenile predator gets choice fish circling river (8)

12 Forlorn thing, replacing love with one (6)

15 Bloody treatment and daily abuse by sibling (8)

16 Fragrant as a nameless Wordsworthian poet, say (8)

19 Sword–shaped sateen creation (6)

21 Artist who sounds cheerful (8)

22 Sporty type of male appreciative of painting etc (6)

24 Here Labour begins true representation in America (6)

25 Inclined to accept roentgen unit study (8)

26 See 22 down

27 Joyful orchids cultivated without state backing (9)

DOWN

1 Newspaper illustrations carrying risk (5)

2 'Quite agreeable, collecting rubbish' (wink, wink!) (7)

3 Large body to go comfortably round, being out of shape (5)

4 Heap laid out, but not a place to land on (7)

5 A second chance for foiled contestants? (9)

6 Rather bleak victory, with lame finish in Test (7)

7 One who takes lives in central development (9)

13 Tennis champion off to the small Italian commune (9)

14 Ground is to alter betting system (9)

17 Beneath mountain peak, diverging trails wind (7)

18 Carbon ring coil associated with a petal formation (7)

20 Refrained from releasing a book that's marked (7)

22,6across,26 Tip waste food over press and sackings are on the cards! (5,4,4)

23 Habit of taking a lot of wine with ice–cold starters? (5)

Solution see page 266

ACROSS

1 Deeply thoughtful, keen to raise issue (6)

4 Perennial reptilian superpower (6)

9 See 23

10 Seen in mirror, something black on bed, mister, a silk stocking (10)

11 Hot wire warmer (6)

12 Cry of frustration opening drink in European city (8)

13 Liquid may start to curdle after utensil used to mix cocktail (6,3)

15,27,25 Evidence of slur after organisation dropping regulation for food, supposedly? (4–6,4)

16 River sport (4)

17 See 3

21 Prod by female failed to deliver clear message (8)

22 Clear horror breaking cover (6)

24 Dash to see groom boarding launch (10)

25 See 15

26 Attractive, I appreciate that man (6)

27 See 15

DOWN

1 Love admitted by champ and companion for genetic engineering, say? (7)

2 Fragrance preceding 18, by the sound of it? (5)

3,17 Might it be one's ultimate dessert? (5,2,9)

5 Trading in Australia terrible, as viewed from down under? (6)

6 Game OK, Celtic having brought in a winger (9)

7 Clever clogs strikes up relationship (7)

8 Club awaiting the law courts, initially wound up (5,8)

14 Comical putting make–up on bear (9)

16 Dog, cat and hamster, for example? (7)

18 Marker pens record European city (7)

19 Wasted time as elfin smut served up? (7)

20 Make a short visit with John and relations (4,2)

23,9 Old traveller in company car with damage in front (5,4)

Solution see page 267

ACROSS

1 Frilly corsets for one hand-medown (6)

4 Make dashing leap, finally breaking cup sure to wobble (6,2)

9 Intelligence? Country that elected Bojo's losing it (6)

10 Is French car maintaining parking rule? (8)

11 Hornblower's hard on a corps pursuing gold coin (5,9)

13 What Victor may take, left in misery (10)

14 Use taser on left-leaning eccentric (4)

16 Honey bee caught in inlet (4)

18 Uproar at home? Smarten up the mess, say (6,4)

21 Scatter articles of Spanish novelist (4,10)

23 Setter heard vessel getting slap on the lid (8)

24 Fine soldiers knocking on walls (6)

25 Maybe Oscar Wilde ate these when out to lunch (8)

26 Dry American statesman who led a coup (6)

DOWN

1 Line on taxi mostly grease (4)

2 Loves magic works, which may be Puccini (7)

3 Lack cake decorating skills when receiving large number of churchgoers (8)

5 Stamping the time when teachers finally relax? (11)

6 Warcraft from America's leader, but so refined (1-5)

7 Former member of RAF moving one's milk (7)

8 2-D shape I'm not sure is for group of plants (9)

12 Give jobs to the boys? Time for a meeting (11)

13 Types info covered by journalist with Time (9)

15 A German with silver ra-ra skirts overturned jelly (4-4)

17 Puts up stakes, fencing badly (7)

19 Most slimy East German admits: 'You can't believe me' (7)

20 Piscine is rather cold (6)

22 Cockney is nowhere to be seen in time of putsch (4)

Solution see page 267

57 Set by Vulcan

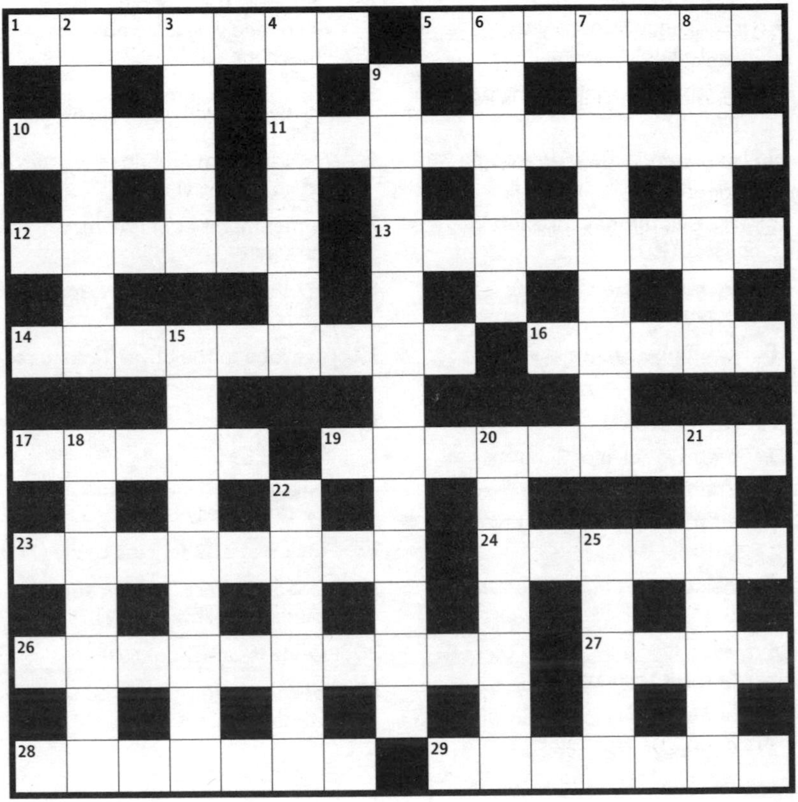

ACROSS

1 Time off is sacred — I had a break (7)

5 One beats by a very short distance (7)

10 Perhaps hawk's attempt to catch rook (4)

11 Gamely implying lawn is inferior? (4,6)

12 Site around area in Kensington, for one (6)

13 Do only mediocre cricketers have these? (8)

14 Odd cardinal has funny ideas for a game (4-1-4)

16 Stupid to put toddlers on this? (5)

17 Fairies showing personalities? Not at first (5)

19 Character that directs one elsewhere (9)

27 Most worrying tooth decay in a way (8)

24 One should not eat more quickly (6)

26 He sells at a knock-down price (10)

27 A throw of the dice rejected in centre of revolution (4)

28 Vegan at first madly ardent to be green (7)

29 Trifling sum for strip (7)

DOWN

2 Paperwork finished without tears (7)

3 Help province up country (5)

4 Stuffy serials need rewriting (7)

6 Assassins who spare women? (3,3)

7 Give voice with opera cast in Asian city (9)

8 Demanding to take dope during leave (7)

9 After rant, head arranged to punish humiliatingly (3,3,7)

15 Hated former editor keeping old car (9)

18 In talk, entice to accept shocking treatment (7)

20 Compel men to go through broken fence (7)

21 Revolutionary spray dispenser (7)

22 Lament hit on head, calling in doctor (6)

25 Take a turn round a kingdom (5)

Solution see page 267

58

Set by Vlad

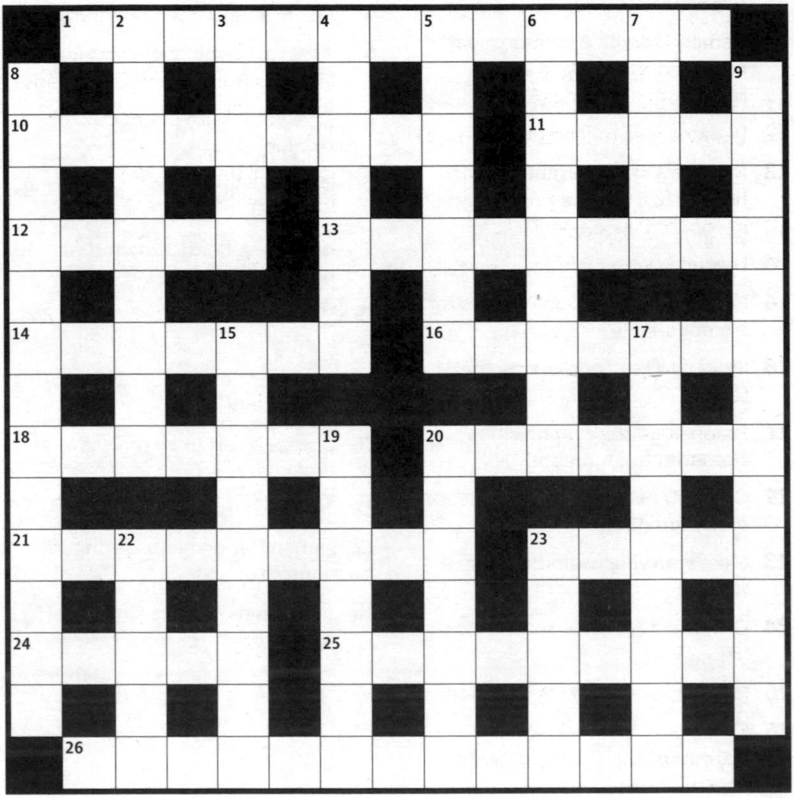

ACROSS

1 Free school meal tiny? Rashford's first to get involved (13)

10 Isn't regularly on guard outside, one's deduced (9)

11 'I shall go first!' — little bossy woman oppressing Vlad, in a manner of speaking (5)

12 Became less ragged after trim (5)

13 Number One hit about Scottish holiday spot — one providing haven for Paul originally (3,6)

14 Left and got picked up (7)

16 Pussy keeps heading for cream? I'm not sure (7)

18 Kicks up fuss about energysaving tariffs (7)

20 Proposition earth mother prepared to embrace (7)

21 County town near London, home to royalty (9)

23 Girl or boy, one's a bit of alright (5)

24 Bounder stealing note, one for the ladies (5)

25 Support post (9)

26 Right-wing faction helping ... for payment! (13)

DOWN

2 Blur faces but nothing otherwise (9)

3 Reduced clergyman's department finally (5)

4 Set off crash dieting (7)

5 Excuses from sweetheart — and address for woman taking part (7)

6 Islanders unhappy deporting duke? Wait and see (9)

7 Food that I arranged — not all of it turned up (5)

8 Enjoy one's job looking after Charlie — secure and trouble-free (4,9)

9 Attempt to discredit press cameraman — pigs! (5,8)

15 Tricked! Root in middle of house of ill repute! (9)

17 Managed to stop one director touching up another (9)

19 So gutted, having killed American — getting put away (7)

20 Maybe roofer eating dates is not a great catch! (7)

22 Rate old Boris — and for Macron that's upsetting (5)

23 Children about to pick up a small furry creature (5)

Solution see page 268

59

Set by Tramp

ACROSS

1 Tramp's clues, ultimately knocked back: awful feeling (11)

9 Left hospital department, soldier returns with round mark on skin (7)

10 Frantically, peer needs potty (4,3)

11 Go through take-home pay? Empty purse first (9)

12 Tickle the ivories: you perform sonata, finally, when retired (5)

13 Change the order in a McDonald's (4)

14 Briefly watch fashions: they're often imitated (4,6)

16 Sewer in the main street runs with muck outside (10)

19 Covers not featuring model's first poses (4)

21 Slip outside from fire after smoke retreats (5)

22 Public appeal put business on strike (3,6)

24 Son having short paddy; it is getting several looks (7)

25 Perfume's no good: smell at the back is rank (7)

26 On which performers stand out: huge stars performing with the theatre, primarily (6,5)

DOWN

1 Shocking and unsafe: LA star moving houses over this? (3,7,5)

2 Film bagging Oscar is not dry (5)

3 Group of drivers carrying very old clubs make green (7)

4 A Greek ordeal: English with nightmare after vacation (7)

5 Carry advanced weapon: acknowledge those giving it up for you? (4,1,3)

6 Unusual crime scene — PC out to get subject (8,7)

7 Excellent tip from sommelier getting drink (4-2)

8 They feed the young and you, we hear, over summers, not initially (6)

15 One allows donkey to get put down (8)

16 It's most wise to decline drugs on start of tour (6)

17 Cryptic puzzles on transport (7)

18 Correct to interrupt senators on both sides: they're involved in Congress (3,4)

20 Bargains in fantastic sales, opening from Thursday (6)

23 Iron everything upside down for man (5)

Solution see page 268

60

Set by Qaos

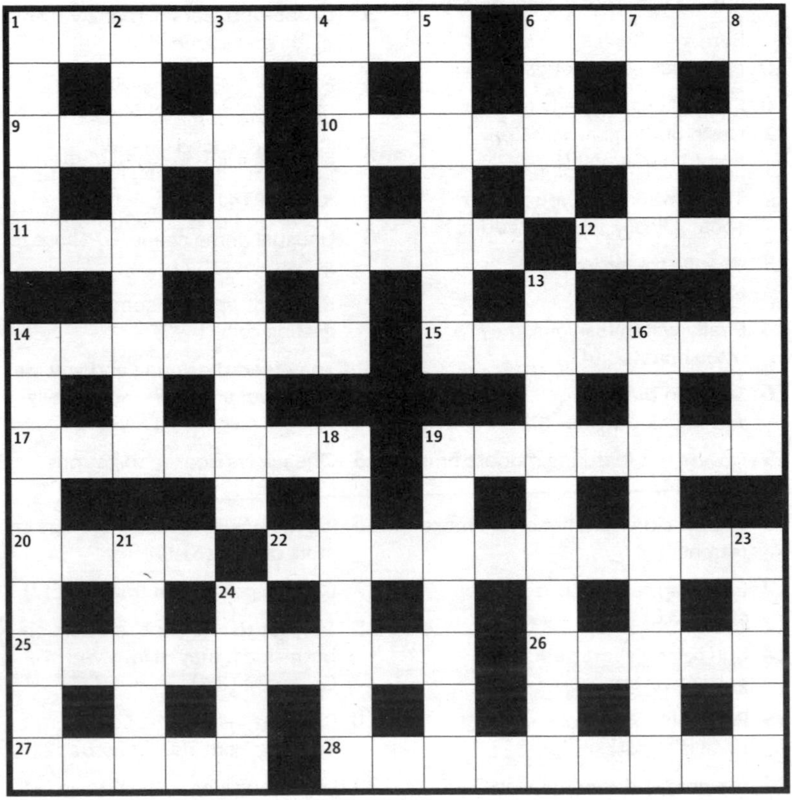

ACROSS

1 Sausage and mash — was butter right substitute for energy? (9)

6 Allegedly, food banks produce little fire starters (5)

9 Bother with a horse, say, otherwise go back (5)

10 Basic gluing regularly for a DIY tool? (6,3)

11 Sends reports of plot discovered in steelworks? (10)

12 Leaders suggest England's ruled by a European (4)

14 Giant bikes require work to replace a bearing (7)

15 Before first kiss, nervously phone fabulous bird (7)

17 Type of irrigation: 99? (7)

19 Jeans exchange hands — initially, elongated stripes become checks (7)

20 Drunk love shut of book small drink (4)

22 Toad, rabbit and sea dog (10)

25 For Penn and Teller, according to Carroll, it's a driving mechanism (9)

26 Film-maker Shyamalan wants opening of movie to be darkness (5)

27 American guitarists have the last word over vote (5)

28 Electrical devices grill her toast on Sunday (9)

DOWN

1 Pound locks up special animal (5)

2 A new setter, I state, is heavenly (9)

3 Cryptically, God in sin? (10)

4 Racing cars like to carry 50 7s (7)

5 Restaurant where Spooner's woman to come first (3,4)

6 Light beer after a drop of pilsner (4)

7 Scoundrel to attempt return, hiding in Paris street (5)

8 Rock bands love sex from behind in isolated environments (9)

13 I never slow cook animals (10)

14 Approximately 1000 top best in revolt — it's a really nasty place to be (9)

16 Longing for battle, lost again (9)

18 Sycophant in slow-moving vehicle (7)

19 Umpire trading iron for titanium — now he no longer works (7)

21 Most annoyed about a little bit of rainy weather (5)

23 Football clothing starts to excite strikers and wingers (5)

24 Capital to be seen during October/November (4)

Solution see page 268

61

Set by Nutmeg

ACROSS

1 Bewildered, did he thirst for gossip? (4,3,4)

9 One Greek character left in time to find another (7)

10 High priest number two holding mass for stricken city (7)

11 Batting pundit ran informal game of cricket (3-3-3)

12 Land cultivation hard on slope (5)

13 Quits flat (4)

14 Hold tailless mammal back pretty quickly (10)

16 Sport available on large rescue vessel (4,6)

19 Snappy greeting between clubs repeated (4)

20 Conduced round home, given internal protection (5)

21 Call round, unfortunately missing member of the House (4,5)

23 Handiest resolute knight sent to the front (7)

24 Arrogance of man averse to keeping uniforms apart (7)

25 Opportunists, one waiting to open morning paper (4-7)

DOWN

1 About to withdraw bill that 21 is known for? (12,3)

2 String of shops alongside beauty parlour (5)

3 End trial with explosion destroying a part of plant (7)

4 Scrap previous wordplay raised as an example (7)

5 Adolescent cheers up dons put in prison (8)

6 'This bed's horrid', says Violet Elizabeth, as story intensifies (3,4,8)

7 Wasn't tempted to interfere — neither Jack nor Jill did (4,4,5)

8 Conservative HQ's prerogative? (5,2,6)

15 Fancy dress mostly ready-made (8)

17 Former filling stations unopened — dedicated people sought (7)

18 Wind resistance in middle of Channel different (7)

22 Look to exploit wretch (5)

Solution see page 269

62

Set by Paul

ACROSS

1 Bath hot, dealer lying back, maybe (7)

5 See 22

10,17 Shape of course about right for figure immediately before square? (9)

11 Cover dirty path frantically, king passing through (5,5)

12 See man again before short journey (6)

13 Builder's coat put on, hold buttons up (8)

14 See 16

16,14 Study in small hotel, say, sustained income (5,3,6)

17 See 10

19 Most definitely gone and done wrong instead? (5,4)

23 Fail to deliver breakfast? (3,2,3)

24 Island, unduly round land (6)

26 Daughter behind vehicle in problem with brakes, initially shocked (6,4)

27 African lions in captivity might go here, did you say? (4)

28 Strange and foolish? (7)

29 Cheat bedding former lover, sordid practice? (7)

DOWN

2 English nation's poor rich kid? (7)

3 Rough pot filled with rubbish, primarily (5)

4 Rhythmic beating of 16 14 (3-1-3)

6 An ecclesiastic residing near Machu Picchu, for example (6)

7 Very drunk, run into item of furniture (9)

8 Italian city isn't built up around area south of walls in Corsica (7)

9 Malevolent woman, mean having severed head, eats Australian native (9,4)

15 Predatory fish from Scottish island a bird cut up (9)

18 Correct number finishing short race (7)

20 Celebrity eating off lap then? (7)

21 African relative carrying wood uphill (7)

22,5 Pretender in stream, gaining benefit in fighting at the front (6,7)

25 Audibly, second note's the first for composer (5)

Solution see page 269

ACROSS

9 Substantial part of secular generation (5)

10 Bold university dean excited about social gathering (9)

11 Party with small jug for friar (9)

12 Catholic leaving continent with undue speed (5)

13 Fabric in front of warehouse stored incorrectly (7)

15 Names for knobs? (7)

17 Extent of place to practise shooting (5)

18 See 16

20 Animal in Italian river good for source of biodiversity (5)

22 Very lawful petition (7)

25 Glazed frame covering top of raked stacks of hay (7)

26 Boost unit in charge (5)

27 Plant pip containing source of protein before spring (9)

30 Element of Japanese comics? (9)

31 Deep-fried potato containing head of minute animal (5)

DOWN

1 Drained fluid from bottom of well in part of garden (4)

2 Slim American operated boat (8)

3 Unusual tea leaving baby with gas (4)

4 Museum trainee getting wine (8)

5 Take off in boat (6)

6 Nothing was new for this new president (10)

7 Tool in bench is electric (6)

8 Side of faceted gemstone (4)

13 Fight police officer in cell blocks (5)

14 Garment with awfully neat crotch (6,4)

16, 18 Closure for team during pause (5,3)

19 Drop weed carelessly into ground (8)

21 Shrub in grand forest on borders of India (8)

23 Stripy designs covering navy fabrics (6)

24 Investigations involving lower part of reproductive glands (6)

26 Member hiding money in book (4)

28 Diner's first to get fabulous fish (4)

29 Run gently from damaged pole (4)

Solution see page 269

Set by Brendan

ACROSS

8 Part — with ease, if broken? (8)

9 Part of greater honesty that's starting to be seen between Swiss banks (5)

10 Idiot getting role after change of heart (4)

11 Part of pageant I'm at — terrific ephemeral stuff (10)

12 Small part of statistical report for firm (6)

14 Part of big issue to be raised in old court — increased rent (8)

15 Formalities progressively reduced, with two parts switched (3,4)

17 Quarter thus includes area for grass (7)

20 Starters for our first part of meal, naturally (2,6)

22 Engine parts — throttles (6)

23 Bunch elected in cunning way to expedite part of bill (10)

24 Final parts in cast recast for theatrical hit (4)

25 Part for Maria Callas to study endlessly (5)

26 Nothing remaining from fire around very cold part of year (8)

DOWN

1,21 Leading man that has two parts on stage (5,3,6)

2 Bewitched, in part, using new spell (4)

3 Brutal, apart from having silver lining (6)

4 Almost back, holding it up as part of the Guardian, say (7)

5,16 List of parts a repairman tossed out (8,8)

6 Direction to players to reduce noise — part of one I composed (5,5)

7 Partly withdraw, making borders of state change and decrease (6)

13 Unfathomable part in Shakespearean comedy? Not so (10)

16 See 5

18 Hear test broadcast in places where many a player takes part (6)

19 Bit by bit, go inside controlling mechanism in parts of country (7)

21 See 1

22 About to depart or part forcefully (6)

24 You may part with this part of fowl (4)

Solution see page 270

ACROSS

1 Like the Ancient Mariner's ship, tide- and weather–battered (4,2,3,5)

9 Refuse to accept bad copy? Yes man! (9)

10 African mentioning child's foot (5)

11 Criminals being executed? They start off being first rankers (5)

12 One enforcing a go–slow emptied water barrel into reservoir (5,4)

13 Character of composition briefly requires pens (8)

14 PC in court opened eyes? (4,2)

17 Private meal changed in second (6)

19 Large amount put on paper in set period (4,4)

22 A month back, foul up badly in it? That's irregular (9)

24 A lot of insects turn to the water to cross river (5)

25 Notice a lady is president twice (5)

26 Fish product is ready to drink? (9)

27 Perhaps church support aeronautics, though something hairy (6,8)

DOWN

1 Girl's staidness cracked: maybe a flare–up (8,6)

2 Fish (salmon) short of some oxygen, caught by a fleet out of area (7)

3 There's no way to break sinful fraud (9)

4 In football move, run faster to leave United floundering (8)

5 Approval as European joins up (6)

6 Took part, having excellent day — about time (5)

7 More than usually insulting, artist chucked press out (7)

8 After fruit drink, book entertains those who like to wallow (14)

15 Slip-up on particular area in speech (9)

16 Sweet I stuff into ill–fitting suit (8)

18 Overcome impudence that holds state up (7)

20 Before a long time, lake lost because of this? (7)

21 Being extravagant with jewellery all over uniform (6)

23 Sage from Dublin I dropped completely (5)

Solution see page 270

66

Set by Crucible

ACROSS

1 Students read this current old diary in Times (7)

5 A short delay in Switzerland leads to complaint (7)

10 Mark awards ceremony, taking sides (4)

11 Charlie stops negotiating drugs course (10)

12 Film posh Young Conservative dancing (6)

13 Annual growth margins excluded insulin supplier (8)

14 Very funny rocks lecturer kept in cupboard (9)

16 Plump person regularly feasts on turkey, apart from innards (5)

17 A lot of sailors secure firm part of mast (5)

19 Check rooms in monastery for controversial sources of therapy (4,5)

23 Hero fell among stars (8)

24 Spot the sack that's put on board (6)

26 Dracula's health indicator? (5,5)

27 Bring up Republican auditor behind back (4)

28 Georgia came across art in French cells (7)

29 Question odd features of ballet during concert (7)

DOWN

2 Fake coins found in Ireland — one's coated in enamel (7)

3 Joely Richardson's helping London theatre (5)

4 Tropical plant, one with large swelling on root? (7)

6 Grave, perhaps, that may reveal one's origins (6)

7 A fine caterer arranged support, following operation (9)

8 Old order to disperse rhino at intervals with sensitivity (4,3)

9 Relish opening a huge English paper that's 16 (7,6)

15 Steroid is working after short time in heart (9)

18 A 22 ordered article in the Listener? (7)

20 Keep watch on idiot in Othello, for one (7)

21 Briefly want sugar magnate to produce food for young (7)

22 Protection in bed? That's old hat (6)

25 Beat biblical epic, getting shot of the Tablets (5)

Solution see page 270

67

Set by Paul

ACROSS

1 Greek poetess with an aversion to fools erasing name on biro? (6)

4 Dissertation not say in essay, described with what we have here (6)

9,16 Approach food items fresh from the frier? (4,4)

10 Vehicle where one after mass transported by people in a ferment (10)

11 See elderly woman briefly reversing pattern in socks (6)

12 Darling behind my back, swoon (4,4)

13 Head bagging new job, I haven't been informed (4,3,2)

15 Dubious humming, intro forgotten (4)

16 See 9

17 In need of repair, some girl pinning a dress up (9)

21 What we do carelessly in writing about an Amercan state? (8)

22 Country cabin in block (6)

24 Engine part with nut on screw (10)

25,3 Actually live (2,2,7)

26 Bill when Charles will reign? (6)

27 Name dividing Washington and Berlin? (6)

DOWN

1 Movement as follows lion stopped by head of zookeepers (7)

2 Musical flower (5)

3 See 25

5 River hot, shade burnt? (6)

6 Sound of setter filling puzzle up for speaker (9)

7 Fine material cut, so lustrous (7)

8 Surrealist dunking fish factory in gin, as weird (5,8)

14 A raft travelling south carrying pieces from shore? (9)

16 Bone crusher ultimately in ferment (7)

18 Tough seafood, starter changed (7)

19 Belt out to bind organ, very painful (7)

20 As well for French and English as English main? (2)

23 On reflection, somewhat grim, a musty taste sensation (5)

Solution see page 271

68

Set by Philistine

ACROSS

7 Nick hugs Maria, mostly a good person (9)

8,26 Chocolate producer from a hundred with a gong in 23? (5,5)

9 You're a loser, says European partner (9)

10 Backstreet securing triumph for Jedward? (5)

12 Underwear market surrounded by paramilitary force (6)

13 Protection from Philistine's beginning to massacre harmony (8)

14 Somewhat reactionary cabinet is bewildered by something in cyberspace (7)

17 Fish supplement pawned? (7)

20 See 11

22 Motto may be 'to consume a type of fruit' (6)

24,25 Anonymous 10 could be in range (5,9)

26 See 8

27 Cliff top, with a fair easterly breeze, as a place to eat? (9)

DOWN

1 Confusion as naughty 11 embraces outgoing youth (6)

2 Functional study shows copper deposit in thick skin (8)

3,16 Decisive assessment essential in disputed titles (6,4)

4 One takes charge of contraceptive method used on Tina Turner (7)

5 Naturalist appearing in calendar — WI, naturally! (6)

6 It's not gross to be into witchcraft, it's attractive (8)

11,20 A memo to NHS unusually features politician and actor (4,8)

15 Essentially deny the dance being revamped and improved (8)

16 See 3

18 It's cruel indeed to be humiliated (8)

19 Rabbits OK to evolve into kangaroos (7)

21 Cutting room ultimately in the red (6)

22 Kind of town Hollywood is giving silent treatment (6)

23 Reporter of fiction here with gang (6)

Solution see page 271

Set by Vulcan

69

ACROSS

8 Impenetrable row of crops at one end of the country? (8)

9 Scores four? Many more (6)

10 Work to do, then, promptly (2,3,3)

11 Philosopher speaking in a crackly whisper (6)

12 One's stocking up, ready for the occasional visitor to drop in (6,9)

15 Boxed in, one has a trying time (5)

16 Request directions, being awry (5)

20 Not really expect to describe Bob's family quarrel? (4,7,4)

21 Run after small girl, who may be on thin ice (6)

23 Mountain originally broken in seven pieces (3,5)

25 Audibly breathe a cunning plan (6)

26 Many distributed our menus (8)

DOWN

1 No working period; time for lunch? (7)

2 How mortgage may be secured free of charge (2,3,5)

3 Crazy about one girl (4)

4 Spotted large number at church in past (7)

5 Miserly girls just avoided accidents (4,6)

6 Are they before or after chickens? (4)

7 Starry artists tell a reviewer's hiding (7)

13 High-level plot for gore and mayhem (4,6)

14 All the same, these letters give a basic education (3,5,2)

17 Factory on holiday emptied and idle (4-3)

18 Grand group of swingers (3,4)

19 Pick one parent as the best (7)

22 Secured change of diet (4)

24 Handle call (4)

Solution see page 271

70 Set by Tramp

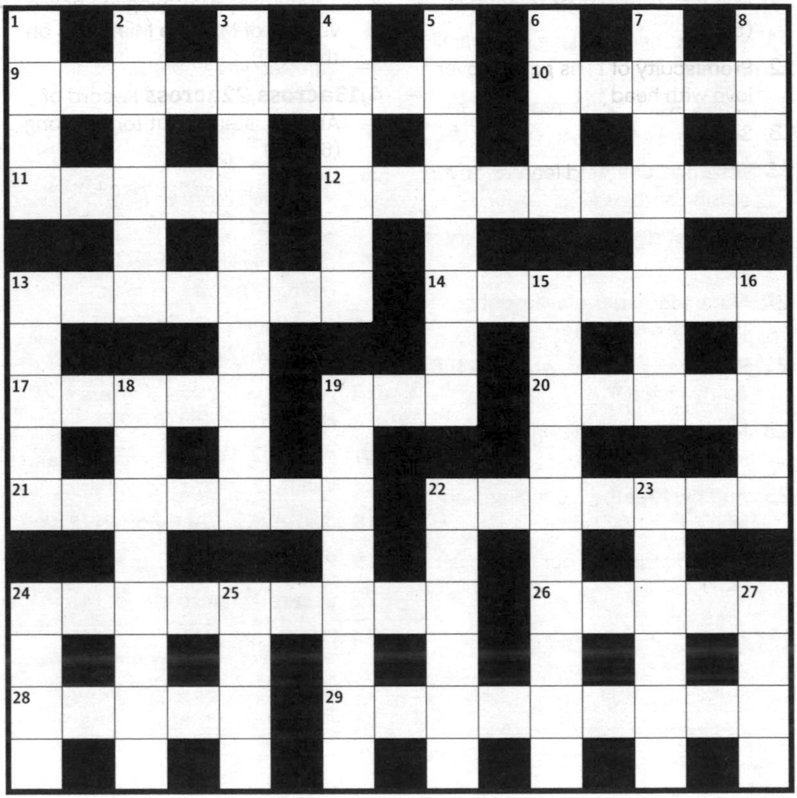

ACROSS

9 Newspaper and music magazine once featuring old timer (9)

10 Playing song live (2,3)

11 French all lining river to get fish (5)

12 Promiscuity of Miss getting over love with head (9)

13 See 4

14 Wise people round learner driver cutting speeds (7)

17 Remove clip from one page, say (5)

19 Abba song mostly average (3)

20 Handy protection's good before passion (5)

21 Release songs for performance without payment (3,4)

22 See 4

24 Crowd get up where musicians play (9)

26 Rows from couples: right to break up? (5)

28 Pile of money, money, money — small amount dropped off (5)

29 The Winner Takes It All demo good: Ring, Ring going to get remixed (4,5)

DOWN

1 Record label tense for release (4)

2 Initially Super Trouper dress is light ... (6)

3 ... Agnetha performing in English version of Mamma Mia dress on this? (10)

4,13across,22across Record of Abba? Listened out for old song (6,4,3,7)

5 One of us upset getting left inside was once bad (8)

6 Turn up, initially taking chance on me (4)

7 Abba song in can following number one? (8)

8 Heavenly bodies in type of blood bank (4)

13 Music tones (5)

15 16 to follow as lights roam around (10)

16 Group from Sweden: time to go over records (5)

18 Dancing Queen apt or The Name of the Game? (8)

19 Woman has sex with affairs (8)

22 Pet fish died: bowl terrible, ultimately (6)

23 Exaggerate, having finished act (6)

24 Hit poor piano (4)

25 Face party (4)

27 So Long, half cut single (4)

Solution see page 272

ACROSS

7 Publicise footwear aid for a diver? (3,4)

8 Attempt by shy little bird (7)

9 Travelled, heading away from Welsh area (4)

10 Broadcaster crosses barrier, becoming a drinker? (9)

12 D-Day beach sergeant's first news (5)

13 Joker and king involved with piquet (spades) (8)

15 International holding of billionaire (4)

16 Round of cards — fast one (5)

17 One's taken by the dancing, not love (4)

18 Possibly an official enquiry from them, as a way to break awkward situations (8)

20 One who can bridle at Americans somewhat (6)

21 Feel rule needs changing about new carbon molecule (9)

22 Canned ham with top removed (4)

24 Promotional gift of loose cheese? Right out of it (7)

25 Wheeler's modest loveless description of low-level celebrity? (7)

DOWN

1 Secret device used with indignation? (4)

2 This allowed pub customers to get stuff off their chest (8)

3 Victoria wasn't a married American journalist (6)

4 Result of a failure to score: cocaine added to a kilo (kg), roughly (4,4)

5 Fools around with large snowdrifts (6)

6 Note about US city (4)

11 Agree Jacquie's certainly guarding this (9)

12 Wader has to keel over after sun (5)

14 Sort of a tree, one seen in refectory? (5)

16 Spice up routine crime, perhaps (8)

17 Care worker's flat support? (4,4)

19 Pedestrian jazz performer left out and replaced by King (6)

20 Drawn to the old kind of patterned cloth (3-3)

21 Passion Tree, associated with ecstasy (4)

23 First bit of stomach fits into opening? Let out pants (4)

Solution see page 272

72 Set by Nutmeg

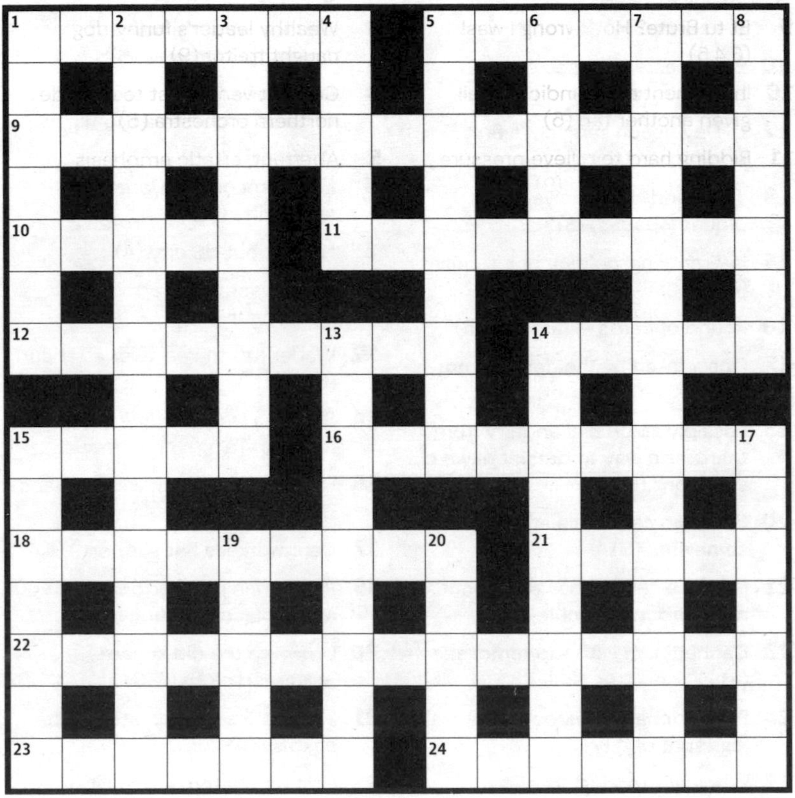

ACROSS

1 Home Office branch last to refurbish fully (2,5)

5 Tenor tackling new work gets support in studio (7)

9 Et tu Brute? How wrong I was! (6,4,5)

10 Instrument could indicate hail, given another tap (5)

11 Bidding hard to relieve pressure in shipping abroad (9)

12 Old fogey rejected dessert and paid (7,2)

14 Piece of metal used for part of joint (5)

15 Base time indicated (5)

16 Bird seed with smoother coating (9)

18 Was single potty adequate receptacle for drinker? (9)

21 Lines adopted by party harden (3,2)

22 Little-used ruling leading to beneficial qualification (2,4,9)

23 Husband picked up reference book lacking top cover (7)

24 Got into line, prepared for a roasting (7)

DOWN

1 Distinct details about superpower (2,5)

2 British artist sculpted duke with alarming hat (4,5,6)

3 Wealthy leader's funny dog caught traitor (9)

4 Concert venue first to exclude northern orchestra (5)

5 Aberrant, erratic emphasis placed on noun (9)

6 Updated drainage system, reversing initial direction (5)

7 Science feature on ancient medicine filling empty pages (8,7)

8 Seemingly removes autograph from drawings (7)

13 Lengths first spanned by balls (9)

14 Depart suspiciously with Nutmeg's media player (4,5)

16 Maudlin knight hampered by desire to follow mum (7)

17 Brooded quietly at home, cutting grass (7)

19 Ball game void without pitch (5)

20 Diocesan council, say, ignoring a show of consent (5)

Solution see page 272

ACROSS

7 Where prisoners eat CO (9)

8 CO appearing regularly in Schroedinger style (5)

9 He made reptiles vanish, recreating past magic (2,7)

10 First seen in Nightingale, undying resilience supporting each CO (5)

12 Inhale from a smoking thing (6)

13 Strange, strange, strange: ultimately CO (8)

16 Where there's a will there's way? Contest disputed, not won (7)

19 Tories' top minister lacking means to gain goodwill for CO (7)

22 Perhaps Cape Fear, Fahrenheit dropped after cold closes in (8)

25 Boatman follows core of convoluted book (6)

27 About to tuck into sourdough! (5)

28 CO scaring me in a funny way (9)

29 Bad-tempered Republican leader ejected by CO (5)

30 Even cycling finds unexpected zeal around united country (9)

DOWN

1 CO allegedly held back with hesitation (6)

2 Time for New Yorkers to eat load of French food (8)

3 Neither thanks mass uprising for CO (6)

4 Stick around a little, because this is sweet (7)

5 Reduce tension in defeat: a tyrant's leadership rejected across America (6)

6 Article about riot appeared (6)

11 See 14

14,11 Reheats damaged part of wood? (3,4)

15 See 17

16 Boatman's origins in the arts reassessed (3)

17,15 Admirer of oddly stupid, yet rugged, prominence (6)

18 CO manifested in muscle oxidation (4)

20 Anonymous newspaper article uncovered abuse by CO (8)

21 Carry on making endless profits (7)

23 Not a major route to CO (6)

24 Drink coming up with Spooner in the vicinity (6)

25 Struggle with editor's extremes in the Spectator (6)

26 Sad lament for inherited status (6)

Solution see page 273

74

Set by Picaroon

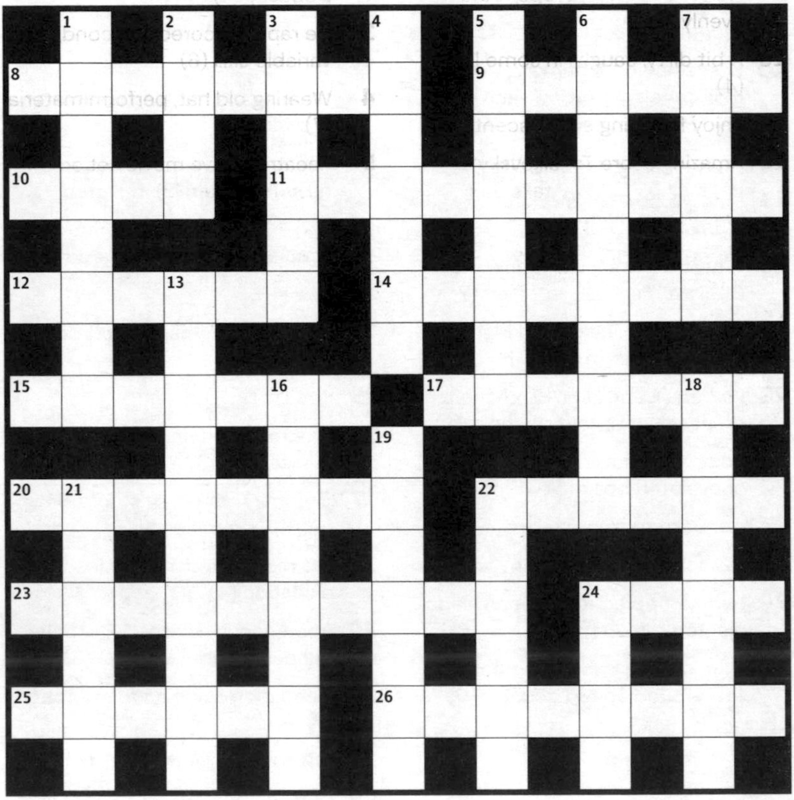

ACROSS

8 Name–dropping singer covers half of aria he scored manually (8)

9 It's used to cook proper cuts evenly (6)

10 A bit dirty, caught in some light (4)

11 Enjoy following sweet scent (10)

12 Amazing score Tchaikovsky's beginning — it may take your breath away! (6)

14 Computing bores rarely represented in books (8)

15 Welcomed in dugout, a venerable English scorer (7)

17 Score that's zero for golfer (7)

20 What sewer did in street caused irritation (8)

22 Score from one of the 19 backing officer (6)

23 What could make us calmer is a worldly notion (10)

24 Top scorer (on and off the pitch) (4)

25 What 8 and 24 put on vessel about to set off (6)

26 Spooner's to stuff seamen in transport (8)

DOWN

1 He often scored century, like a star (8)

2 Scores piece, finale from Debussy (4)

3 He rapidly scored a second, with variable skill (6)

4 Wearing old hat, perform material (7)

5 Theatrical love movie set around eastern desert (8)

6 Shows impatience, admitting tramp doesn't know the score? (5-5)

7 Create a vibrato effect as part of a score (6)

13 Score synthetic meth and use thus (5,5)

16 Tries to cut peonies periodically put in black vehicle (8)

18 Composed score without previous blemish (4,4)

19 They try to score total: it's divided by a hundred (7)

21 Score which is doubled in cricket (6)

22 French scorer has butter and drink at home (6)

24 Set of loaves? With no time, he produced scores (4)

Solution see page 273

Set by Carpathian

156

ACROSS

1 Suited worker crossing river (6)

4 Quiet time/times embracing old attendant (7)

9 Seamstress initially having skill and independence in exam about tailoring (9)

10 Trips over foot barriers, spilling whiskey (5)

11 Male employs goddesses (5)

12 Close family member the French rejected after a short time (9)

13 Party lines a republican originally supports for cash (7)

15 Son and I can second protests (3-3)

17 Enquires about missing one rook and other pieces (6)

19 Disagrees with man during teaching session (7)

22 Abstemious office worker's energy and speed (5)

24 Excellent, but half-hearted, meal (5)

26 Smears heads of business leaving under reprisal-free system (5)

27 Drove from school with magazine director (9)

28 Former partner has hot drinks and puffs (7)

29 Way a sun exists in a constant state (6)

DOWN

1 Warmly embraced somebody endlessly, improperly (7)

2 Treats dog with drug and a bit of sympathy (5)

3 Satellite picture of map once so distorted (9)

4 Controls parasites in post offices (7)

5 Blunder made by manager losing final piece (5)

6 Fraction of hot blini cooked with bit of lox inside (9)

7 Yankee interferes without mass agreements (6)

8 XXX Ken Loach film about income support and society (6)

14 Braggart's showy entrance (9)

16 Passenger transport crossing space in passing (9)

18 Late meetings, as scene changes (7)

19 Beats Charlie a lot (6)

20 Teams crossing middle of district in steps (7)

21 Balanced knife on head of louche earl (6)

23 Take a selfie, holding frame for support (5)

25 Crushes record held by Manx cat (5)

Solution see page 273

ACROSS

1 Paul's online flimflam (3,4)

5 Heavy metal band's flamboyant front man (7)

10,8 As fine white powder may be initially snorted, lifting spirits? (4–7)

11 Juggling not right, as entertainment frightening children (5,5)

12 Pirate almost stealing gold coin (6)

13 The moment has arrived where winger tackles relative after greeting (4,2,2)

14 Show a dye liberally applied to lid in essence — here? (9)

16 Hollowed out, nothing inside old red fruit (5)

17 Impact, by the sound of it, reversed in experimental psychology (5)

19 Work on set is requiring effort after evidence of blow (9)

23 Spectacles in time slipped into Bill Gates's trousers? (8)

24 Underperforming? A poet (6)

26 Capital of Louisiana in answer, one gathered? This isn't! (3,7)

27 Portion including a carrot (4)

28 Pop star back in country garden (7)

29 Covering area, look for New York running back for New York team (7)

DOWN

2 Decorate article that's boring too (7)

3 Do well in filing of a report (2,3)

4 Progenitor concealing eye colour (7)

6 Need one in charge when head is sacked (6)

7 Ultimately verboten to wear Speedos, say, for members of the clergy (9)

8 See 10

9 Party hearing about delivery groups likely to provoke argument (13)

15 Prep done by hybrid tool inspiring an early settler? (9)

18 Dummy put on crate, briefly (7)

20 Country one visits while I head northwards (7)

21 Drink on top of wardrobe featured in feast (6,4)

22 Visitor to bank, perhaps, left in indignation (6)

25 Polish child almost flipped over puzzle setter (5)

Solution see page 274

ACROSS

9 Writing that could make me propose — a contradiction in terms? (5,4)

10 Thomas, poet and Nobel Prize winner (5)

11 Is inclined to delete nothing from pieces of poetry (5)

12 Wildly romanced, clutching English or Italian love stories (9)

13 Nasty European immersed in ten gallons, perhaps (7)

14 Washed over front of crowd gathered together (7)

17 Indulge, oddly, poetaster's ending — his work's limited (5)

19 Dedicated lyric to listeners that's outstanding (3)

20 Untrained old volunteers retreating in conflict (2,3)

21 Reveals our country's introducing new degrees (7)

22 Harsh about replacing author's final piece (7)

24 Genuine article installed by company that signals danger (4,5)

26 Cut that 3, when split and reassembled (5)

28 Patriarch named in a chapter in part of OT (5)

29 Rhyming slang, say, is included by US author, male (9)

DOWN

1 Starts off every poem in collection in style of Homer (4)

2 Boy with fishing gear, eg lines set on Westminster Bridge (6)

3 Poetic structures in novel serve in support of text (5,5)

4 French composition from Byron — delightful (6)

5 Is the speaker on type of TV friendly? (8)

6 Source of first introduction that rhymes? (4)

7 Humorous bio priest cut and cut (8)

8 Ascribed source of many rhymes before long (4)

13 It's found among 3, with fixed syllabic structure, similar to this (5)

15 Radio station's broadcast about reading — and writing? (10)

16 Elegy, say, cleared up (5)

18 Fruit put on heap — one concerned next clue but one (8)

19 Nameless constable demolished barrier (8)

22 Old man disturbed in tree (6)

23 One upset about verse is completing stanzas (6)

24 Lots of islands having female dotty characters? (4)

25 Quartet's initial scheme for 2, perhaps (4)

27 Frost's old–fashioned poem (4)

Solution see page 274

ACROSS

1 Left before decision, creating divided opinion (5)

4 Caesar, perhaps, in his day and age had one with Antony ... (8)

8 ... where you may learn Italian couple is due! (8,6)

10 Reposition the panel, revealing frequently overlooked room feature (8)

11 Force bank to provide short term storage (6)

12 Nervous types could set something off (9)

15 Picking up waste after performing is pure tedium (5)

17 Following instinct, director proceeded carefully (5)

18 Cleaner finds it is more sensible going outside (9)

19 Perfect place for turning one vessel covered in gold (6)

21 Singer entertaining queen, for example, reveals a different side (5,3)

24 Defeat prior to engagement? Things aren't so good after that (4,6,4)

25 Some armour Britain lost in dreadful gun battle (8)

26 Exercise illegal occupation (5)

DOWN

1 Use revolting fabrication — it could help you sound believable (6,6)

2 Sea creatures captured using little spears? (9)

3 Ask for money from hoodlum exchanging grand for cocaine (5)

4 Private enters petitions for new recruits (9)

5 Remove one's used sweaty tank tops (4)

6 Criminal ran brothel, mostly obscene (9)

7 What a wandering poet thought lacking company is obscure (5)

9 Old slip made of superior substance, perhaps (6,6)

13 Graduate lecturer pockets big profit from game (9)

14 Highlight a short low–scoring innings? (6,3)

16 Film of nature's most unusual bloodsucker (9)

20 Men following car to get this type of work (5)

22 Straightens out partners following initial mate (5)

23 Inform on these local extremists (4)

Solution see page 274

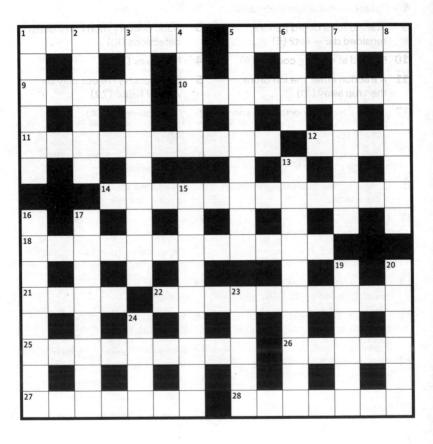

ACROSS

1 Fellow leads firm sailor on board (2–5)

5 Relative size has girl worried (7)

9 Start to roll a board game's tensided die — set? (5)

10 Excited at nearing country (9)

11 A fraction enter the inn drunk, then run away (10)

12 Learner breaks sports equipment like this? (4)

14 Huge shock! Nostromo alien — can none get lost? (12)

18 Some expert activity, right, like hang-gliding? (7,5)

21 Took drugs, thought to blow money (4)

22 Dessert from South Africa prepared in a globe (10)

25 Art seldom ruined by him? (3,6)

26 Traveller to welcome Terry inside (5)

27 Excellent! McCartney's being broadcast (7)

28 Regular beans with poor diet wants a vitamin! Tempted? (7)

DOWN

1 Trick by one stealing gold crown (6)

2 Chairs in cars (6)

3 Adult delivery men carry ones defections (10)

4 Room key (5)

5 508 (roughly) reject play on words? Relax! (7,2)

6 Call inquiringly? (4)

7 1 + 500 + 10 + 50 etc translated into personal speech (8)

8 Wonderful cat, just not ordinary (8)

13 Shape of diamond strangely altered to save money, including copper (7-3)

15 Historical role player's career not flourishing (2–7)

16 Vague sense to gather up American lubricant (8)

17 A shoe size bigger than 9C, say, on conference goer (8)

19 Because I'm travelling skywards, the speed of light is enormous (6)

20 Hit sung loudly after dropping out (6)

23 One's avarice has no end, yes? (5)

24 Author kept spinning plate (4)

Solution see page 275

Set by Puck

ACROSS

1 Drawer once containing office PC? (4,9)

10 Removing contents of new Audi with long name (9)

11 Reddish-brown start to autumn, in two different ways (5)

12 Last to use vehicle's a Welshman (5)

13 Get gripes regularly: content's missing from supermarket with most small branches (9)

14 Type of spirit, sort served alongside wine (7)

16 All but first of fires put out leading to charge, if put out again (7)

18 Longing for women, if lust unbridled (7)

20 Finery of sporting gear worn by boxer (7)

21 Bloomers in game against Premier League side (9)

23 Two characters going after 1 (not Turner) in shop (3,2)

24 Bottled water that's still the first drunk by 12 mostly (5)

25 With eight sides in National League heading for administration, first month has past (9)

26 Cyclist of note about to sell his pants (4,9)

DOWN

2 What 1 used get mixed in a pot still, periodically (3,6)

3 Approaches Arsenal about wanting a midfielder (5)

4 Didn't include synonym for 'hand' in dictionary (7)

5 Horse, one sporting queer ears more inclined to droop (7)

6 Carrying out transfer of a second new player? (9)

7 Left part of church in decline (5)

8 Heroic twin brother of princess tormenting us with We Three Kings! Really? (4,9)

9 Poet that's written book on composer (7,6)

15 Rubbish prison, said dissenting voice (9)

17 Pils drunk by nurses? Shock horror, for some (5,4)

19 One searching smallest room, say, for complaint in the Observer (7)

20 Prize crossword compiler needing oxygen intake after cycling (7)

22 Educated girl eating a yoghurtbased side dish (5)

23 Stiff, cold and unfeeling? Not at first (5)

Solution see page 275

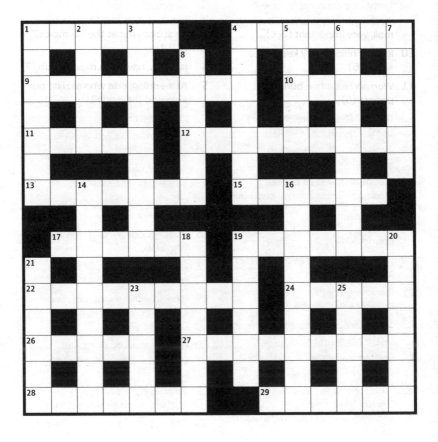

ACROSS

1 Husband of Florence? (6)

4 Tiny amount of French potage given to prisoner (7)

9 While speaking glanced through mail, very important (3–6)

10 Initially heavy duty keeps one sharp (5)

11 Woman has a fine bundle of papers (5)

12 Diamonds, for example, young girl put on smart dress (5,4)

13 Fearful of such a breakdown (7)

15 Give the impression of a very quiet listener (6)

17 Detectives chase sailor to a police box (6)

19 Censors prominent headlines (7)

22 Minuscule coals were blown about (5,4)

24 A despicable man about to pocket one bit of bling? (5)

26 Star name, one adopting fashionable diet (5)

27 Publicly expose talent I've wasted (9)

28 Daughter is to take care of balloon (7)

29 Gateman finally grants admission (6)

DOWN

1 Changes at home and goes to bed (5,2)

2 Bog plant in small border (5)

3 Fabulous time when we were so successful at the Olympics? (3,2,4)

4 Is angry, having to move shrub (7)

5 At wedding, one who assists our side and the bride? (5)

6 Cleans out revolting government office (9)

7 Condition that is barely noticeable (6)

8 End of play is baffling (6)

14 Agrees law needs modifying to show true value of packet (4,5)

16 One may be suited by this second short journey through wood (9)

18 Deprived of exciting adverts (7)

19 Aeroplane makes bouncy noise, full of echo (6)

20 Figure cathedral is majestic (7)

21 Perhaps Russian editor worked hard (6)

23 Woman is a bit more needy ... (5)

25 ... and a bit distant (5)

Solution see page 275

82 Set by Pasquale

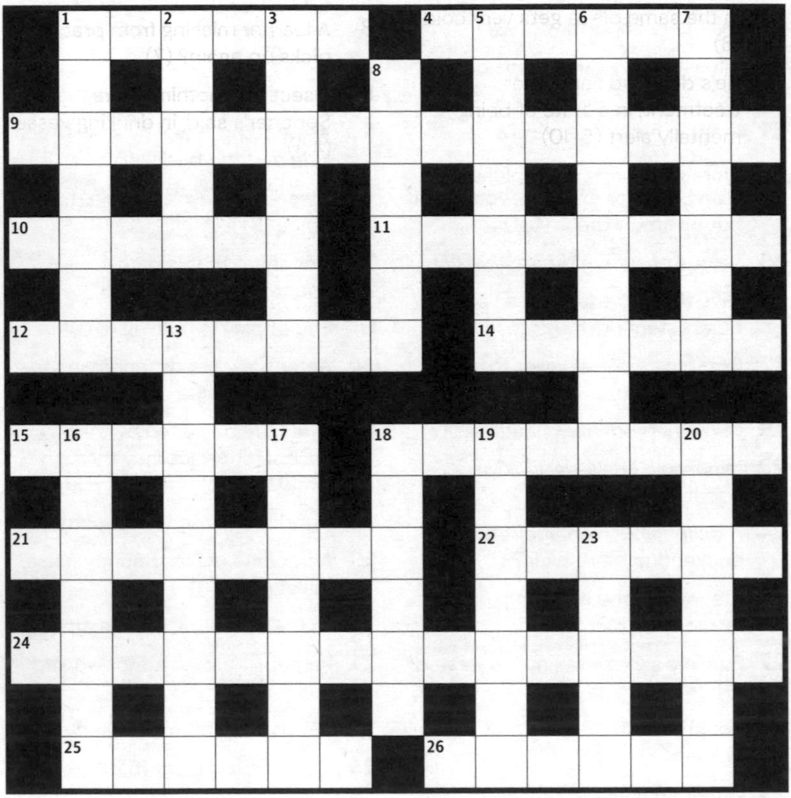

ACROSS

1 Father about heartless performance: 'It's supposed to be funny' (6)

4 More than one mountain creature in the same place gets very cold (6)

9 He's declared sane after treatment, in a state of being mentally alert (5-10)

10 More work here, more pleasure here? (6)

11 Like some roads with bit of confusion — two traffic lights but only one right! (8)

12 Dense group of trees in which little son hides (8)

14 Fellow, one left being given time inside, shown to be this? (6)

15 Portraying an image of a type of chemical bond involving carbon (6)

18 Trees we'd chopped in small areas of land (8)

21 Roman emperor, hiding in enclosure, secured position (8)

22 Spy on street creating trouble (6)

24 Ban duke? Squabble about some rehashed stuff (6,3,6)

25 Idiots in European port missing an entrance to shipping (6)

26 Ogle, needing to grab companion? Well he might! (6)

DOWN

1 Mess made by quiet group in school (7)

2 Take a walk, parking vehicle first (5)

3 A learner missing from practice picks up again? (7)

5 Insect and nothing more, Spooner's said, in drinking vessel (4,3)

6 New income set to provide a small amount of money (9)

7 Half the people looking to catch us have a sneaking feeling (7)

8 Militant Millicent, reportedly one turned on by Americans (6)

13 Officer studies information, schematically presented (9)

16 Queen being grabbed by womaniser in court game (7)

17 Draw together as in an intimate photograph (5-2)

18 On a bike, one's headed North, East or West? (6)

19 Some Eden with love gone, abandoned territory (7)

20 Misery of endless want keeping the old man in (7)

23 Irish water in sunless bog (5)

Solution see page 276

ACROSS

8 A basis for prayers (4–4)

9 Round bag (5)

10 Sailor Bill opens two consecutive letters (4)

11 At first sight, a campfire's about to engulf one (5,5)

12 Neatly replacing one with daughter, Merry (6)

14 Keeper likely to get a buzz from a new strip to go over international one (8)

15 Put out drugs for trials (7)

17 In the outskirts of Los Angeles, snake passes for fish? (7)

20 Infection of one's darling — getting one shot (8)

22 Rock group members' initially short tempers (6)

23 Black–eyed Susan, environmental activist and international ace (10)

24 Has old bowler possibly arrived at end of pitch? (4)

25 Wife is a printer? Shows she's not being serious (5)

26 Dodgy dealer goes in back way for sewing machine parts (8)

DOWN

1 Stranger from France reorganised IKEA on return (8)

2 Aim at spot at centre of token (4)

3 Surgical procedure means life and beginnings of prodigious sex — yes! (6)

4 Hair transplant claim involving setters? (7)

5 Asiatic cooks taking cocaine for painful condition (8)

6 Disparaging term for a medium asteroid orbiting round America (5,5)

7 Rockers possibly making church appearances (6)

13 Astute, missing nothing, considering disorder (10)

16 Placed in centre pile: 'Psychological Recurring Attacks' (8)

18 X–ray unit or back specialist hospital department's information (8)

19 2 in 100 Poles have a duty to go inside (7)

21 Native American doctor, one who favours war (6)

22 Treacherous types: racers, perhaps (6)

24 Said to be a conflicted character's mask (4)

Solution see page 276

84

Set by Vlad

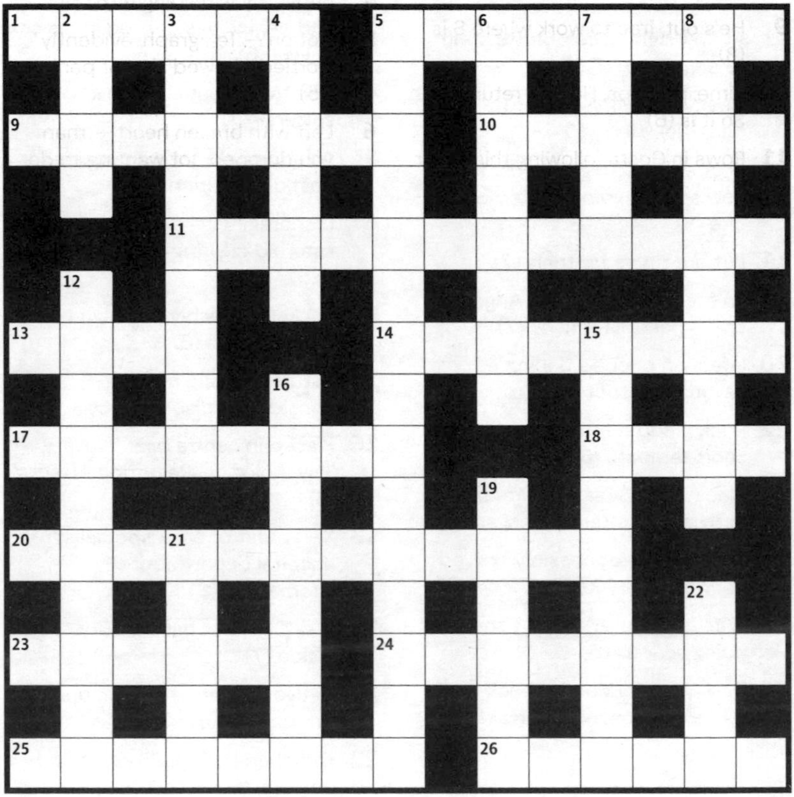

ACROSS

1 Vice squad heartily entertained — say no more! (4,2)

5 Position not conducive to firing CO? (4-4)

9 He's out, free to work where 8 is (8)

10 Time, perhaps, Hamlet returned? So it is (6)

11 Rows in Costa following this order (12)

13 Finishing early, read up on boss (4)

14 An achievement, of course — yes, picked up a good looker (5,3)

17 Runs through a tunnel breaking out (not yet discovered) (8)

18 Mysterious travellers returned from occupying country (4)

20 Main treatment centre (8, 4)

23 Fury over Rex playing a stage villain (6)

24 Suddenly got nasty with a small number (6,2)

25 Heading off, one subsidising fellow journalist short of fare (8)

26 Repeat right away what's left (6)

DOWN

2 Spoils look of tin-openers (4)

3 Deal inappropriately with the Wolverine State (9)

4 Little boy is holding it (6)

5 Not on — Telegraph, evidently worried, showed sign of panic (15)

6 Left with broken heart — man you dumped not wanting to do anything (8)

7 An animal in bed (one having taken Viagra finally) (5)

8 Child one is longing to lift up to secure access to Santa? (7,3)

12 Strangely resonant — it is loud (10)

15 'Stuff it!' — Queen unhappily entertaining Johnson (9)

16 Crooked aristocrat caught — one beyond redemption (5-3)

19 It should be paid daily (gets 50% off) (6)

21 When there's no actual fighting, he's great in the gym (5)

22 Presenter short, so had to show up (4)

Solution see page 276

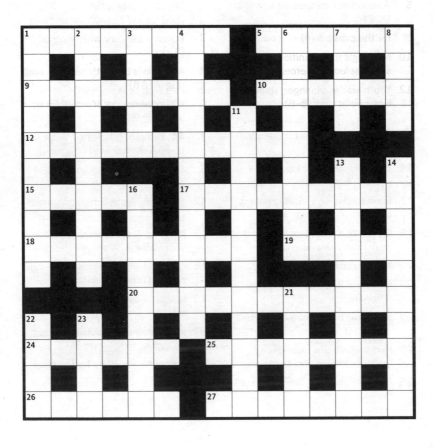

ACROSS

1 Bulletin from channel framing health centre (8)

5 Scratch cricket side on call (3,3)

9 Against cutting identical notes for the present (8)

10 Nutmeg's theme initially missed, showing lack of perception (6)

12 Youth leader's clanger, shielding internee at port (5-6)

15 Drastic reduction in sales oddly overlooked (5)

17 Union to scale down working during month (9)

18 Leave layer covering ancient temple (9)

19 Some specified article plugged by seaman (5)

20 Place for father to hide heiress, with plot brewing (7,4)

24 Caller from US contrarily set out for another meal (6)

25 Person writing schedule substitutes second half of month (8)

26 Propitious start for government in African country (6)

27 One reveres Ireland's foremost injured soldier (8)

DOWN

1 Keenly awaiting release of a poem by PhD in translation (5-5)

2 Guy briefly retained by Touchstone to keep watch (5,5)

3 Follow a century with another (3,2)

4 All there is beneath fertiliser staff dug in (6,6)

6 Potential source of wealth in new normality? (5,4)

7 I blundered, needing ultimately to go up backwards (4)

8 Feature, primarily pretence or reality? (4)

11 Wouldn't part with sole weapon that's proved trustworthy (4,4,4)

13 Work slicing sausages for game participants (4,6)

14 Kind person like Vlad once a Guardian worker? (10)

16 Virtual trade exhibition shortly visiting London suburb (1-8)

21 This lady's going to Hull (5)

22 Pilfer item from nativity scene (4)

23 Scheme taken up by venal politician (4)

Solution see page 277

Set by Paul

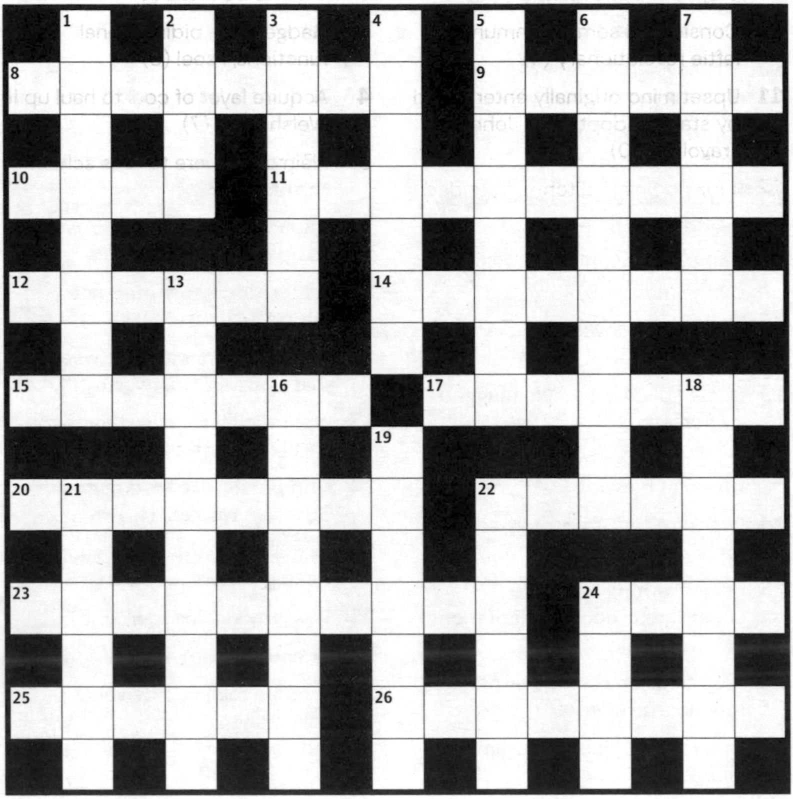

ACROSS

8 Lily, girl accommodating retired soak (8)

9 State where I invested in cereal crop, wasting capital (6)

10 Considered some communist, leftie revolutionary (4)

11 Upset mind originally entertained by stance adopted by John Travolta? (10)

12 Tank ending in ditch surrounded by rubbish (6)

14 Fixation on facial organ as going down, currently? (8)

15 A sticker brought into play, nice one! (7)

17 Classic music genre rejected by Roosevelt, briefly (3,4)

20 Asian rarely seen collecting post (8)

22 School punishment element observed in silence (6)

23 Artist reportedly removed a wheel clamp close to the ground? (5,5)

24 Day book's last prayer (4)

25 Splitting trousers from behind, weapon ultimately exposing blubber (6)

26 Meeting relations (8)

DOWN

1 Christmas attire: appear with this when half-cut (drunk) (5,3)

2 Possession of Scotsman in fact likely to be lifted (4)

3 Gadget with bidirectional functions, I see! (6)

4 Acquire layer of coal to haul up in Welsh town (7)

5 Plain city where tailless school cat raised (8)

6 24 down 10, doctor operated to save skin on thigh (4,6)

7 Alcoholic drink is cradled by server, uncorked? (6)

13 Sinners supposedly recollecting dead man in prayer (4,3,3)

16 Too much fine drinking upset minister, getting sick (8)

18 Generosity in affectionate act inspiring promotion of close relation, finally (8)

19 Look again, as wreck uncovered hell! (7)

21 Wicked queen on phone (6)

22 Mole in crotch, by the sound of it? (6)

24 Indicate evangelist (4)

Solution see page 277

ACROSS

9 Artist and daughter wearing relative's fashion label (5)

10 New title about way of working provided recurring theme (9)

11 Light–fingered types with permission to interrupt meals (3,6)

12 Dance by graduate following sport (5)

13 Steel drum keeping time with first of trumpeters in procession (7)

15 Police search for suspect in flowering garden close to Parliament (7)

17 Plant obscured by yellow heather (5)

18 Setter leaving bread to go off (3)

20 Person in group dropping money in dying fire (5)

22 Door is swimming around inland in a chilly part of the world (7)

25 Staff allowed to get something to eat (7)

26 King at end of extra pilgrimage returned with eastern prince (5)

27 Old nurse close to commode encountering aroma that's characteristic of old age (9)

30 Recommended article leaving drink to editor (9)

31 Bit of wood glue (5)

DOWN

1 Exact replica of small fruit stone (4)

2 Aggressive speech by playwright carrying a fake gun (8)

3 Chap partial to Nottingham ales (4)

4 Move a lever to get lift (8)

5 Failed to find sea surrounding island close to Rhodes (6)

6 Clever clogs right to get drink during strike (5,5)

7 Wings of swan covering dull part of flower (6)

8 King of Mercia once listened to proposal (4)

13 Captives welcoming year in this part of Wales (5)

14 Tremor caused by dessert wine (10)

16 Card for sailor to turn over? (5)

19 East European given piece of butter to turn into culinary paste (8)

21 Official report of headless chicken in container (8)

23 Crikey — jack held by boy playing against Spain (2,4)

24 Judge trading shilling for time in estate (6)

26 Substantial addition to pure alcohol (4)

28 Part of window made from special wood (4)

29 Son deserting post, as appropriate (4)

Solution see page 277

Set by Picaroon

ACROSS

1 High passage diva is struggling with cut (7)

5 What's left on, the electricity supply? (7)

9,10 Bishop isn't dignified gatecrashing function (5,9)

11 Under threes dancing round newspaper boss (9)

12 Colourless layer on fringe of arras (5)

13 Brainbox outspoken in row (5)

15 Poorly, one way or another? (2,1,3,3)

18 Loose family members one's seen in lodge (9)

19 Brilliance of recital, cellist making a comeback (5)

21 Chicken backing away from gangster (5)

23 PM's silver ring and Chinese dresses (9)

25,26 Dance groove captured by rockers' material (5,4,5)

27 A little baby's sallow from a very deep bed (7)

28 Dirt Conservative's found in shoe (7)

DOWN

1 Service vehicles from Italy, it's said (7)

2,22 Wild social do — put easy chair away (4,5,5)

3 Say back Caesar's last words to Brutus? (5)

4 Hands on man's bum during prison time, sent up (9)

5 Soldier breaking free is not yielding (5)

6 Steed in novel Emma is to run badly (9)

7,17 Woman rejected current husband, getting together with Harry Barker (5,9)

8 Rent out foxy clothes in serious fashion (7)

14 Turning up to fix eg mink or fox coats (9)

16 Many a chronicler shrinks in recital (9)

17 See 7

18 One's purple in bed, if such frolics end in angina (7)

20 Being so might make performance of lute fun (7)

22 See 2

23 Is a Liberal permitted to barge in here? (5)

24 Where ratings are lost (2,3)

Solution see page 278

ACROSS

4 Place to make a note of profit (6)

6 August and another month almost fun, nice in the middle (8)

9 Not so wild about beginning to play fiddle (6)

10 Storyteller assembles great universal catalogue (8)

11 'Hwyl fawr', as they say in the Valleys (11)

15 Wooden crown is no good to Peter (7)

17 Country extra worthless to Scots (7)

18 Final decree organised area of the EU (3-2-6)

22 Reaction to jolt in nonupholstered carriage? (8)

23 Strokes substantial ego (6)

24 Choose a path in abstract (4,4)

25 Bleed a corrupt minor official (6)

DOWN

1 Incline to keep at home, as wine may be on offer (3,3)

2 Territory's head welcoming a southern European (10)

3 Horse in stud's outside, glittering (8)

4 Encourage work on car that is inclusive of tax (8)

5 What goes on in bed repels me, unfortunately (3,5)

7 Hallucination is no end of nonsense (4)

8 Appealing to reduce noise at the back (4)

12 Chief constable is a venomous creature (10)

13 Dancing in red fez, extremely agitated (8)

14 In vehicle, husband once left half-cut: has he gone to Monaco? (3,5)

16 Tease cracking obsessive up leads to actual laughter in court (8)

19 Firmly established as England captain? (6)

20 Be up against an objection (4)

21 Journey back in seconds from ski resort's train station (4)

Solution see page 278

ACROSS

9 Regroup behind mountains (9)

10 Brewer's agent definitely saves a ton (5)

11 Australian and Yankee hosting finest PM (7)

12 In middle of power cut Republican gets shock (7)

13 Late spin doctor carried in current up north (5)

14 Education graduates quietly study cover at night (9)

16 Test for dentist before and after qualifying? (4,11)

19 Labelled each book stolen by cardinal (9)

21 Jam one drug inside another (5)

22 Replacement chopper unwisely turned east (7)

23 Scream one's stifled at church crush (7)

24 Wife comes in behind Labour (5)

25 Game girl tours part of the UK, a fabulous place (9)

DOWN

1 Item in trunk you are missing in British seaside resort (10)

2 I ate crab at sea, hence my indigestion? (8)

3 Medic works on last bit of nasty complaint (6)

4 English sailors expressing a feeling of resentment (4)

5 Instant victory over Germany renewed strength (6,4)

6 Help revolutionary over variable period in US (8)

7 Taste last bit of tuna in dish (6)

8 What irritated viewer during last year? (4)

14 Boycott poet harbouring European buccaneer (10)

15 Ass died carrying leader (10)

17 Withdraw two women university introduced (8)

18 Rewrite ruling on former respiratory aid (4,4)

20 Send up note for producer of junket (6)

21 Shakers film set in vineyards (6)

22 Record first half of find (4)

23 Very old 8, for instance (4)

Solution see page 278

91

Set by Paul

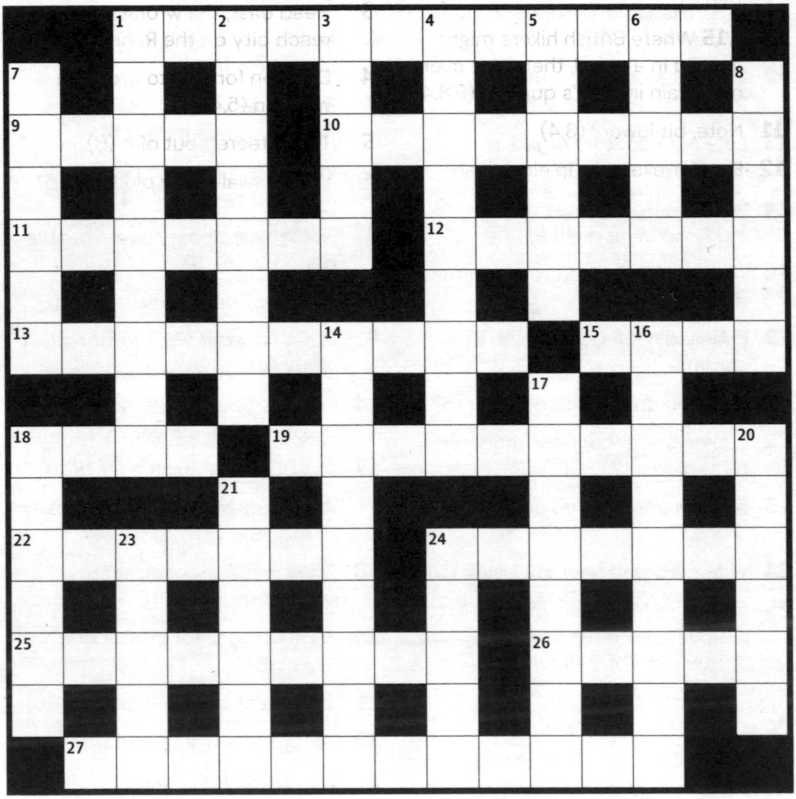

ACROSS

1 On blacklist, a so-called piece of music, creation of 22 (12)

9 Chick egg, by the look of it, left in rain (5)

10,2,15 Where British hikers might go wild in a wood, then race over mountain into 22's quarry? (9,8,4)

11 Note, bit lower? (3,4)

12 Fire, for example, in electrical component? (7)

13 Tango in ballroom dancing, women's ultimate hit? (6,4)

15 See 10

18 Character also falling sick after Jack? (4)

19 Punch buffoon, grabbing bully from behind, creation of 22 (10)

22 Wheels turn for author (7)

24 Pasture in impermissible scene (7)

25 Vessel like that burning midnight oil, dash of paraffin thrown in (4,5)

26 Talk hosted by professor, a teacher (5)

27 Bond cuddling girls, sex not entirely judged fairly (4-8)

DOWN

1 In political draft, article time after time referring to two parties (9)

2 See 10

3 Head east, the wrong way, to reach city on the Ruhr (5)

4 Draw on fortune to produce weapon (5,4)

5 Total steered out of it (6)

6 Whale swallowing old boat (5)

7 22's menacing beast mopping up duck and orange juice with sponge (6)

8 Black music, for example, in order for composer (6)

14 A lot bad, so a lot to repair (9)

16 Previously mentioned area, if so shabby, beginning to decay (9)

17 Laid up, search the internet to secure a fantastic job, wonderful for 22 (8)

18 Island captured by ordinary chap is worth a chortle (6)

20 Bubbly ruler in 2 15 (6)

21 22's very sharp, very sharp ultimately in test (6)

23 Track source on the telephone? (5)

24 Soothing word, razor initially having cut you once (5)

Solution see page 279

Set by Brendan

ACROSS

5 Position of bishop and cardinal making one become angry (3,3)

6 Act the wrong way, cutting precious tree (6)

9 Leaders in White House the reverse of smart in Washington — what's the downside? (3,3)

10 Weapon in novel Pale Fire (3,5)

11 Heads off tippler's excessive alcoholic tendency, attachment to bottle (4)

12 Something sailor needs at that point covered by one side of bridge always (7,3)

13 Set piece — it's spelt out, as you can hear, in the other across solutions (apart from 23) (7,4)

18 Leaderless, is deaf — his thing is what'll diminish schools? (3-7)

21 Quick removal of initial no-no for doctors from pharmacy (4)

22 Notice changes after English left democratic process (8)

23 Exactly 50% of disease in one area, part of Europe (6)

24 Live in endless childhood? Certainly! (3,3)

25 Anxious, having no time to get Chinese manual (1,5)

DOWN

1 Tranche of boodle in sterling for Irish quarter? (8)

2 Give in first place with pained expression (6)

3 Harpies gallivanting about, like other mythical creatures (8)

4 Less composed editor fighting American over royalty (6)

5 That is to say, arranged help for arduous trek (6)

7 Races one can't complete (6)

8 Entering a quiet city, changed into shades (11)

14 Old man's daily crosswords etc (8)

15 Refer to work Greek character turned up that's prosaic (8)

16 In fact, join a new league? (6)

17 Playing in position as substitute (6)

19 If upset, put on such varied neckwear (6)

20 Problem with equipment, needing good fruit pruned (6)

Solution see page 279

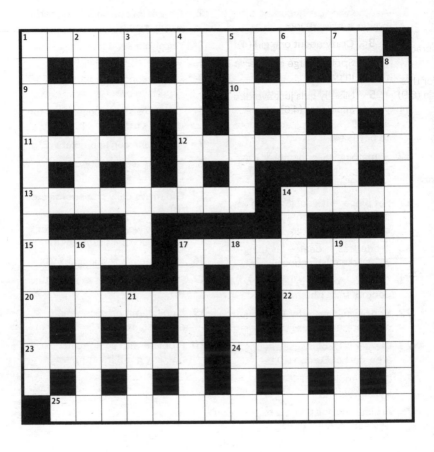

ACROSS

1 Yo-yo game ceases to worry; win or lose, I don't mind (4,4,4,2)

9 Lard costing nothing? Is this the healthy version? (3-4)

10 Tea, a little butter, and one piece of bread (7)

11 May she look after girl in empty nursery? (5)

12 Court calendar shows one hoping to be accepted (9)

13 Working in parlour perhaps, go at it, not bothered (9)

14 Make fun of American for rejecting sweetener (5)

15 Heading off north and east at first on river that runs into the Med (5)

17 Extremely happy a garden cultivated this? (9)

20 One under ten confused by legal deed (9)

22 Edge past farm animal, to pick this? (5)

23 Some explore, leisurely, a fabulous Rhine feature (7)

24 Wholemeal, we note, has high temperature inside (7)

25 Is it criminal, being made to stand in line here? (8,6)

DOWN

1 Embarrassingly ghastly French kid? (6,8)

2 Material arranged to cover a container (7)

3 Crack about the ears? It'll bring a groan (5,4)

4 Freely I stream their wonderful music-making (7)

5 Artwork that's not initially attractive (7)

6 Seat in church where one keeps an animal? (5)

7 Good marks for preparing cheese (7)

8 I prove agnostic about cake (8,6)

14 This is how senior bishop runs a TV programme (4,5)

16 Given strict instructions to be tidy (7)

17 He was bound to prove entertaining (7)

18 Gradually fade and have to be brought back for burial? (3,4)

19 Fabulous Greek girl dined during festival (7)

21 Only prepared new material (5)

Solution see page 279

ACROSS

1 Fellow, having an edge, lost it (7)

5 Two males producing cloth (7)

9 The lowdown on class (5)

10 Commercial vehicle put in remote connections for rural housing (3,6)

11 Assent to treaty accompanied by noises off (9)

12 Vitamin helping blood to clot stops skin peeling (5)

13 Garment tenor's wearing split from behind (5)

15 Joiner employed in B&Q (9)

18 Beaten entertainer that is eliminated could be contestant again (2-7)

19 Shed containing old sink (5)

21 Outdoor seating area with 50% in occupation? (5)

23 Unorthodox types of bonsai spreading across border (9)

25 Confusion as I turn right, going left, in limbo dancing (9)

26 Nick to get off the mark (5)

27 August report largely devoid of content (7)

28 Old Greek city king rejected urgent appeal by child (7)

DOWN

1 Lighting for short stay under canvas, deluxe style? (3,4)

2 Local church admitted to previous naivety (9)

3 Yankee invading force endlessly seeks victims (5)

4 Trouble dividing a mother and son upset spiritual leader (5,4)

5 Live piece started (5)

6 Officer casing area dismissed for taking unrefined coke? (4-5)

7 A seaman entertaining Nutmeg served up Indian dish (5)

8 Army medics checked out and took a stroll (7)

14 Whispering wino needs to articulate 'I must go' (5,4)

16 Implement used on farm to topple branch (9)

17 Eccentric soul madly pursuing an unclothed woman (9)

18 Stitches up army engineer mates (7)

20 Have control of backup groups carrying spades (7)

22 Iodine injected in rather twisted part of leg (5)

23 Stop knocking back drink in past (5)

24 Those starting modestly in speed event perform badly (5)

Solution see page 280

ACROSS

1 Turned incognito after role, essentially avoided identification (11)

9 City developer rebuilt our slum (7)

10 This will shed light on gang engaged in crime (5-2)

11 Fancy ritzy cars like those in lockdown? (4-5)

12 Took steps to depose king in full (5)

13 Stop weirdo letters (4)

14 Second Greek character, intellectual and imposing (10)

16 Here is game with drunken groom about to wake up (6,4)

19 Confront what's been kept under cover during pandemic (4)

20 Middle of Viennese bonbons, round and plump (5)

21 Aide could provide estimate (5,4)

23 In a clumsy way, one gets plenty wrong (7)

24 Change a sphere into a cube? (7)

25 Agree with boss to go after desktop when nobody's around (3,4,4)

DOWN

1 Mausoleum feature is yet undecided (7,2,2,4)

2 Missing the odd school disco is a pain (5)

3 Police try to bury dodgy tapes (7)

4 Philistine, a broadcaster with the university? Unbelievable! (1,3,3)

5 Broke in and disturbed Rupert (it's in the papers) (8)

6 Detectives finding information on bed with rope around its end (3,8,4)

7 Lacking 19 1 across possibly, apropos the rise of first-rate aria (13)

8 Pure red tea stirred by a French man or woman (13)

15 Short and sweet, not worth changing, so approved (8)

17, 22 Then slowly rue friend welcoming Harry's clue? (5,2,5)

18 Perhaps Sue overworks (7)

22 See 17

Solution see page 280

Set by Picaroon

ACROSS

5 Foreign nobleman and ruler on horse (6)

6 Attack right back stops posing no threat (6)

9 Left-wing militants rejected a suit jacket from Norma (6)

10 Where cars race about madly, dashing at intervals (8)

11 Ironstone in social gathering (4)

12 Overture from Fauré playing, then I hear scale (10)

13 Eager man is in Guardian presses producing a Berliner version? (11)

18 Breed of pet rat eating pork pie wife brought around (10)

21 Genuine article returned broken by Charlie (4)

22 Miss one buried in funeral ground (8)

23 Half-heartedly mouth entertaining answer for emperor (6)

24 Left-leaning parties saving time where men were detained (6)

25 Regime change in places with extremes of temperature (6)

DOWN

1 Too inept to move like a ballet dancer, perhaps (2,6)

2 Amount to part of a whole account (6)

3 Says with stammering tongue, primarily? (8)

4 Money maintains company known for flying fortress in Africa (6)

5 Judge present Times journalist to be doomed (6)

7 Code cracked by unspecified number of people in a group (6)

8 One on board managing rough treatment (11)

14 Patron Saint oppressed by a menace abroad (8)

15 Most wanting to stop working in tense shifts (8)

16 Dangerous creatures in lingerie business, at first (6)

17 Repeatedly say nothing about heartless executive? How exasperating! (6)

19 Brown coats unusual for top Democrat (6)

20 Remind people of lecherous fellow getting ahead (4,2)

Solution see page 280

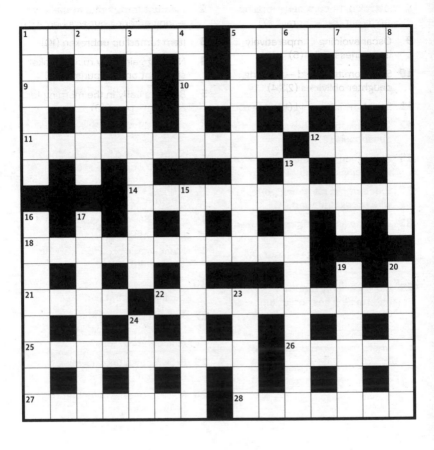

ACROSS

1 What's not real? Defending habit, I'm saying it is (2,5)

5 Comic patter not right — starts to make tasteless crack (7)

9 Oscar avoiding comparatively humourless artist (5)

10 Safe from the flood — keeping daughter oblivious (2,3,4)

11 Sex? Nothing doing! (10)

12 Vale! Leaving disheartened, having failed (4)

14 Wrong! Isn't that easy going round now (4,7)

18 Meal that, for Spooner, needed something alcoholic (6,5)

21 Vlad crosswords reportedly finish off country (4)

22 Royal 'leper' under pressure — he's not himself (4,6)

25 Damon in fix around college and university (9)

26 Cancel culture's ending? Heartless construct (5)

27 Comedian's back, one with incisive material (7)

28 Coming on, tries to be inventive (2,5)

DOWN

1 Working method required to cover large part of course (6)

2 Flourish of trumpets at the start — king entering queen's home (6)

3 Item turned up unbroken (10)

4 Nothing gained by rustic cricket shot (not one for purists) (5)

5 8! That's early in the morning for some into raves (9)

6 Next time — what about November? (4)

7 On record join Bread singer (4,4)

8 Accept some money for watch (4,4)

13 Like changes round pub — they work on the surface (10)

15 Telling crook about books (probably stolen) (3-6)

16 Leave home carrying penny metal fastener (5,3)

17 Event in Illinois accounted for uprising (8)

19 Bundle of energy upset a lot of the same nurses (6)

20 Suspend band on radio (6)

23 News in Brussels on current malaise (5)

24 Hard to stop virtuoso for long (4)

Solution see page 281

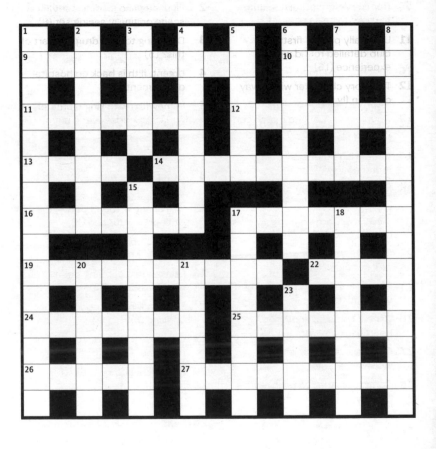

ACROSS

9 Working score to capture hearts — skill around this? (9)

10 Dance and drink: pub closing early (5)

11 Unusually par the first: golf club detailed round without experience (1,6)

12 Toy Story character with a way one can fly (7)

13 Couple from website match.com (4)

14 Cycling gear's allure: ride when excited (10)

16 Stopped unknown American that's gutted — beat badly boxing (7)

17 Comic hero is about ordinary one rowing (7)

19 Unchanged by Times? Papers tempt one, surprisingly? (10)

22 Goddess lives on island (4)

24 Get rid of old joke, perhaps, for a comeback? (7)

25 Men with single publication recalled one model in paper (7)

26 Problem children (5)

27 Chat in party, taking number from nurse (9)

DOWN

1 A serving icon playing — fourth ace in set? (5,10)

2 Film man and leading couples in scene originally seeing set (8)

3 Do wrong to take drug on start of this? (5)

4 Urgent, filth is back on hospital department (8)

5 Disney film with king ultimately replacing leader over a nation (6)

6,8 Creepy-crawly dead at the bottom: saw bizarre _____ in reduced Aldi ripening bananas (9,9,6)

7 Spike prankster's drink (6)

8 See 6

15 One carrying writer on board — one working on plane? (9)

17 Player in bar with supporter (8)

18 Service expert welcoming Queen's total defeat (8)

20 Model after topless sex show (6)

21 Tip: go over with it (6)

23 Important part of bible for homophobe? (5)

Solution see page 281

ACROSS

1 See Englishman about cuts (7)

5 Easy on Prince Andrew? (2,5)

10 Tone from this straight trip (1,2,1)

11 1 getting Tesla — bet he crashes! (3,7)

12 Human ethical argument finally accepted (6)

13 Careless hit and run (8)

14 Spooner gets B, D#, F# permutations from these instruments (9)

16 Endless Jesus raps from the east? Take a break (5)

17 Gem that's mostly white or pink with green sides (5)

19 Senior officers kiss cheek (5,4)

23 Starting with impenetrable vacant stare, reported appearance of US Mafiosi (4-4)

24 Sounds coming from reactionary and half-hearted session (6)

26 Best not to open this farm — no cows unfortunately! (3,2,5)

27 Some monosaccharides get desiccated (4)

28 Prevents tooth enamel defects (7)

29 Abundantly rocky planet, last in galaxy (7)

DOWN

2 Result of using tight controls on Middle Eastern leaders (7)

3 State half-time wager (5)

4 Dish including T-bone (7)

6 Single, appearing for the first time, extremely arty, after love ... (3-3)

7 ... and portrayed as shy (9)

8 Purity of peas cultivated by relative (7)

9 Disease from Eastbourne, say (7,6)

15 Prohibit a clone being developed in this city (9)

18 What about mine? A quiet final tribute (7)

20 Boot wearer, upset about closure, takes off (5,2)

21 Work ethics to welcome mathematical chief boffin (7)

22 Get the better of idiot joining higher education establishment (6)

25 Matilda's mature figure (5)

Solution see page 281

Set by Pasquale

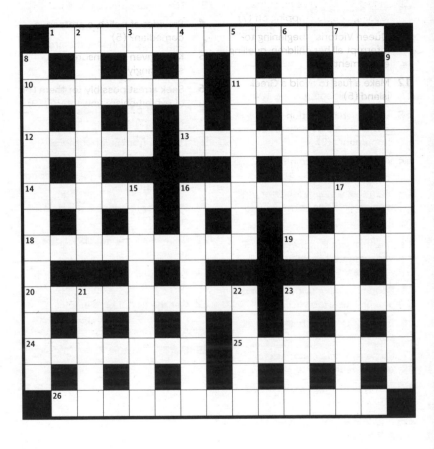

ACROSS

1 Stitched up, like this puzzle? (6–7)

10 Singer Woody gets naughtier, leading couple stripping off (7)

11 Queen Victoria's beginning to interrupt all her children, quelling excitement? (7)

12 Make a fuss to avoid a Greek island (5)

13 Whatever suggestion that was given to Adam when new animal appeared? (3,4,2)

14 Riverside resident in provincial group (5)

16 See list that includes one regarded as a revolutionary hero (9)

18 Restriction coming over time — it is an eye problem (9)

19 Aboard ship hurry to provide launches (5)

20 Bishop falling into lake in African country like a shot? (9)

23 European report of border activity? (5)

24 Row in world of Roman Church (7)

25 School physics unit facing ruin (7)

26 Very exciting Scottish team — super! (5–8)

DOWN

2 Like Derby, plainly? (2,3,4)

3 Boat is exposed, shipping gallons (5)

4 Provider of polish, a grotesque comedian? (5)

5 Kicks given no censure surprisingly (9)

6 Seek arrest possibly for them (bit of exhibitionism unwanted?) (9)

7 Choice of letter size for keyboarder (5)

8 Feature of the gods not being concerned with supposedly lesser mortals? (13)

9 Desert region has near waters diverted (7,6)

15 Statesman sees Libya torn apart (4,5)

16 People coming back see as a result of this instruction? (9)

17 Native attempts to trap British on island (9)

21 Overlooking North American lake is a nest (5)

22 How one may lie in party game, stutteringly (5)

23 Cold climb posing problem for athlete? (5)

Solution see page 282

101 Set by Puck

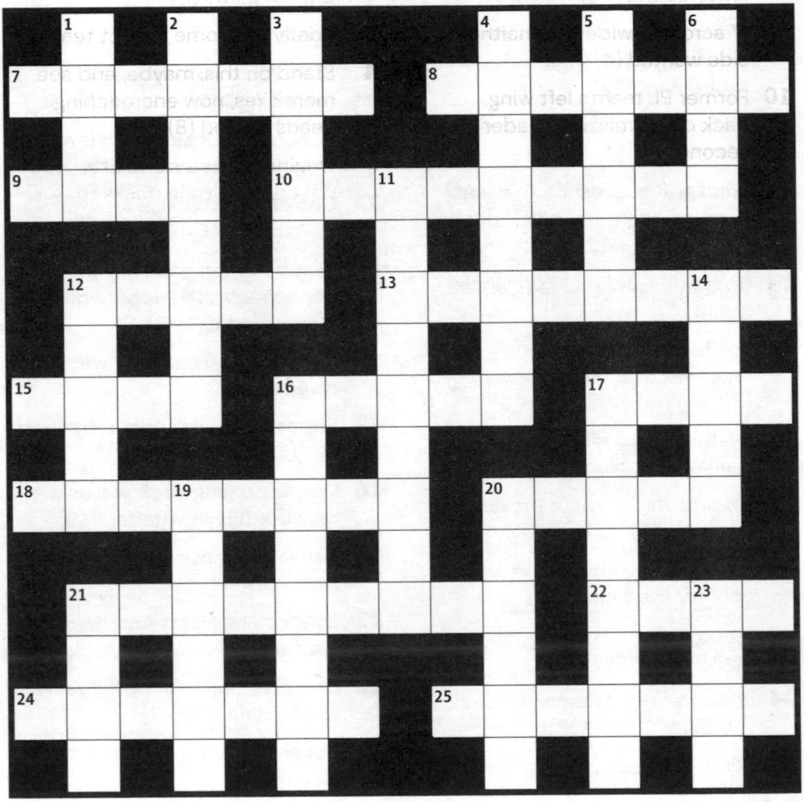

ACROSS

7 Smooth passages of play set goal in motion (7)

8 After losing first point, nervously receives this? (7)

9 17 across, a wide man neither side wanted (4)

10 Former PL team's left wing back dives, missing header and second

12 across? (9)

12 Rubbish dances by Strictly star (5)

13 Detective suffering derision from press team (8)

15 A delay put back festivity ... (4)

16 ... the 25th one, perhaps, for Puck? (5)

17 Academic official content to provide answers (4)

18 Can perhaps shoot game here? (8)

20 Retiring Bengali vicar's wellmannered (5)

21 Streetcars, buggies or slowmoving 3? (9)

22 Some Penguin 'Football Facts' (4)

24 Sadly bicker about who's first to give name for an Antarctic glacier (7)

25 Roy's header really annoys 3 (7)

DOWN

1 17 across having doubled lead, end result is tight (4)

2 Bloomer showed up, leading to one-all game (8)

3 Briefly run some cricket team (6)

4 Stand on this, maybe, and see more? Yes, now encroaching heads shifted (8)

5 Originally all versions of it described sitting ducks (6)

6 A team lacking women in some area (4)

11 Cooked pig liver, edible starter? That's right (9)

12 Times article on current 'right' way to travel (2,3)

14 Slow-paced, lazy speech after tie lost (5)

16 Warning forward respectfully, this may be tugged (8)

17 Little milochlor makers, half of Devon's swimmers (8)

19 Second team's inside men in charge (6)

20 Laid-back Corinthian's teammate? (6)

21 Watched part of play broadcast (4)

23 Conveying charge from governing body, with rule essentially being ignored (4)

Solution see page 282

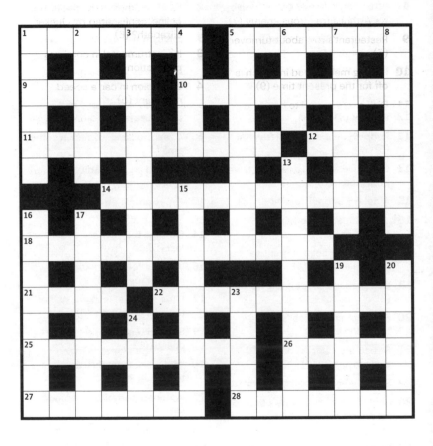

ACROSS

1 Constable's disillusioned with sweet king (7)

5 Miles commanded English to go for Arthur's traitorous enemy (7)

9 Restaurant's row about turnover (5)

10 Putting melted lead in starch is off for the present time (9)

11 Dish that's bound to be revolutionary (6,4)

12 Drink noisily, not softly, and speak without distinction (4)

14 Name associated with band at Wells, a remote community (5,7)

18 Hymn bringing wonder to good group of people (7,5)

21,26 Brand, possibly unusual for a can, is 'Martyr' (4,2,3)

22 Promotion of MP with rent-free accommodation (10)

25 Critical conservative capital about to lead uncontrollable movement (9)

26 See 21

27 Sentry spilled last of the oily liquid (7)

28 Country hotel's masked ball (7)

DOWN

1 To make over an attractive person is rather eccentric (6)

2 Fancy clothes, fashionable, end of line, confiscated by Quaker Elizabeth? (6)

3 It's instrumental in coral gas production (3,7)

4 Champion in car, a speed merchant (5)

5 Puritanical sort of curmudgeon needing internal examination? (9)

6 See 7

7,6 Climber gets talkative with wine (8,4)

8 Misfortune to remove lock? (8)

13 A queen embraced by darling Dicky (10)

15 Wild cat (tiger?) at edge of jungle — potential killer (9)

16 Before the game, coach takes transport (8)

17,24 Doris's musical disaster at start of the year, taking on lead in Evita (8,4)

19 Put old record in missile and take off (6)

20 Plaster crops up on bed almost (6)

23 Relating to the centre of reorganised state (5)

24 See 17

Solution see page 282

ACROSS

1 Fishy sanctuary for a lot of Americans? (3,4)

5 See 17

10 Fishy weapon? (4)

11 Where local workers are detained (6,4)

12 Sounding hard, nothing has replaced one chapter in something easy (6)

13 Soldier on set I look to knock over (4,2,2)

14 Bone goes with third of fillets, fishy Italian dish (9)

16 Middle Eastern city in Doha, I fancy (5)

17,5 One gliding along, fishy pupil at Eton, say (12)

19 Targeted by marketing strategy, left shambolic extremists initially in command (9)

23 Fishy water? Helper on the way (2–6)

24 Fishy weapon? (3,3)

26 Central circles with rings around — might these be flowers? (10)

27 Predator catching egg layer (4)

28 Deception, fishy fizzy drink? (7)

29 Mannerly, fishy chap? (7)

DOWN

2 Reaction, by the sound of it, when apartment evacuated and I go away! (7)

3 Tart up, on prodding feather once? (5)

4 Second river crossed in heading on — point of no return? (7)

6 First of orders signed — sounded like Napoleon? (6)

7 Dump in African capital with English religious job (9)

8 Material originally sewn into each frill, one of two pads (7)

9 Dramatic Irishman secreting fishy weapon? (13)

15 27, for example, wife found in location of canal (9)

18 9 recognises king, these days the vagrant (7)

20 Divine number and letter mentioned? (7)

21 Follow fast runner, then slow (7)

22 Flattened garden ever rising, to some extent (6)

25 Vessel unknown, number spoken by U–boat crew? (5)

Solution see page 283

In celebration of 20 11 12 19 across

ACROSS

9 Thin soil yielding metallic element (4,5)

10 Late bloomer, briefly behind (5)

11 Exposed as ladies with a seedy past? (5)

12 Bizarrely, an opening for 11 digger provides job in growth area (9)

13 Conflict over replacing article in shed (7)

14 Believes book about fungal growth (7)

17 Key work by artist that's a bit of a nut (5)

19 One making regular entries in diary? (3)

20 Earth turned rapidly, we hear (5)

21 Surreptitiously leave what today's lady could have taken (4,3)

22 Retiring poet (not a skilful writer) (7)

24 Assess the situation, having deadheaded pot plant (4,5)

26 Serving of 28s is a likely source of fibre (5)

28 Cut selectively, purging fruit (5)

29 Enough said about Beth working out 11 (2,3,4)

DOWN

1 Women's backsides in border unnerve and frighten bird (4)

2 Flighty males finally returned tools for today (6)

3 Young Murphy used to make others supply a dope test? Nothing in that (4,6)

4 Frozen stiff after first of frosts (6)

5 Reluctant to house youngster? Here's one who does (8)

6 Heard Stand 11 is empty (4)

7 One provocatively removing weeds? (8)

8 Carrier handy today as Romeo has to pull on clothing ... (4)

13 ... coarse garments, luvvie, such as 2 go after? (5)

15 Source of manure applied sparely for fast grower (3,7)

16 Singular blade for cutting marsh plant (5)

18 Identify hedges beginning to require transplant (5,3)

19 Bloomer by lawyer taking raised hat off (8)

22 Sioux pick up good inside information (6)

23 Frontal display aroused dissent and division (4–2)

24 Smart operator hoarding booze (4)

25 South London police going north to make arrest (4)

27 Get up from the ground, oddly ignoring oldie with pink organ (4)

Solution see page 283

Set by Vulcan

ACROSS

7 It is customary to cook a halibut (8)

9 British soldiers capturing East German city (6)

10 Disastrous direction to go (4)

11 Language of Castro bore translating (5-5)

12 The next reign after Louis XVI? (6)

14 A very long time to make a ring (8)

15 Turned to church as an authority (6)

17 In a week or so city goes to ruin (6)

20 In serious outbreak criticise bungling medic (8)

22 After good notice obtain appliance (6)

23 Showing acute intelligence after a strop? (5-5)

24 Weapon that somehow combines power and lots of energy (4)

25 Open to bribery, one is held pardonable (6)

26 A funny reaction in gales, perhaps (8)

DOWN

1 Slack? If not interested, you couldn't ___ (8)

2 Failed to hear the weather (4)

3 What's this on my screen, I hear one swearing (6)

4 Old boy has a couple of teeth to eat fish that's out of date (8)

5 Nigeria had ordered a sound investment (7,3)

6 Extremely rude over a meal (6)

8 Fat monarch makes room for food (6)

13 Where the merry men gathered for a letter? (5,5)

16 I lose mac, awkward thing to wear (8)

18 Pinned into wrong desk? Used to be (8)

19 Write badly with small stroke (6)

21 Very surprised these days to go round part of Hampton Court gardens (6)

22 Turning up in drinking vessel, notice mineral (6)

24 Send back some stale chocolates (4)

Solution see page 283

Set by Carpathian

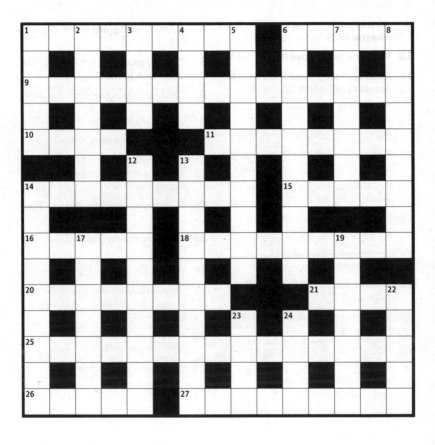

ACROSS

1 Reads grid, wrongly showing neglect (9)

6 Entertains multitudes (5)

9 Foolishly presenting pearl to investor (8,7)

10 Regularly downplays exclusive (4)

11 Abandoned European souvenir in outskirts of Detroit (8)

14 Savage female promises to accept returned Apple component (9)

15 Colour of old church, not quite red (5)

16 Is able to return home without me for food (5)

18 Greyish brown grease ruined clothing (9)

20 Fuss by half-hearted mob is precious (8)

21 Returned plans for tinned meat (1)

25 Make provision for nice cat aunt took abroad (4,4,7)

26 Fish regularly sense ciphers (5)

27 Went down in action involving special constable before finale (9)

DOWN

1 Dance record leading to love (5)

2 Queen after time is a charmer (7)

3 Spot English agent (4)

4 Relative is haggard — not good! (4)

5 Gloomy journalist returning to be dealt with immediately (10)

6 Centaur's daughter somehow ran off (10)

7 Newspaper angle for swimmer (7)

8 Press agitated about hotel serving watered-down drinks (9)

12 Whale upset by one caught in crazy gymnastic performances (10)

13 Good antique piece of tableware initially declared secure (4-6)

14 Amazing fizzy drink gets a lot of criticism (9)

17 Saw Charlie secured (7)

19 Provide a detailed account of old money (7)

22 Dirt around middle of step becomes softened (5)

23 Adopt a pseudonym to cover exploits (4)

24 Smart leaders of American college hiding expenses (4)

Solution see page 284

ACROSS

1 Article in Times left unfinished without a herb used in soups (3,4)

5 One feeds three queens (7)

10 It emerges from opening a 12, initially (4)

11 Drink left over in group refreshed army (6,4)

12 Parent drinks a gin, disposing of one big bottle (6)

13 Tin in hamper, second container of 25? (8)

14 Leader to lead with three articles (3,6)

16 Pale Guardian covers bestseller with renewed energy (5)

17 Carpet that is ancient, small and austere (5)

19 Fruit in soft drink that's oddly part of 9, maybe? (9)

23 29's wi-fi picked up bang outside (8)

24 Cat grabs a radio's top sound producer (6)

26 PM devouring every island's dessert (5,5)

27 Almost completed northern range (4)

28 From memory, boy's gutted, given red card (2,5)

29 Cook stepped around lobster for one (7)

DOWN

2 A very old poster in firm's green (7)

3 Most of French paper's yellow (5)

4 Coach unable to accommodate male, 16 (7)

6 Cite a fruit extract that's talked about by some (6)

7 Colonist guzzling new prince's dairy product (9)

8 Austere English composer's blocking film (7)

9 Battered dish? He loathed it on toast (4-2-3-4)

15 Result of eating too much beef? (9)

18 Transport about half of veal where it's sliced? (7)

20 Staff regularly asleep? It's the drink (4,3)

21 Cross to put outside old Islington pub (7)

22 Seethe a short way into series (6)

25 A carpenter from the south put away nearly new wine (5)

Solution see page 284

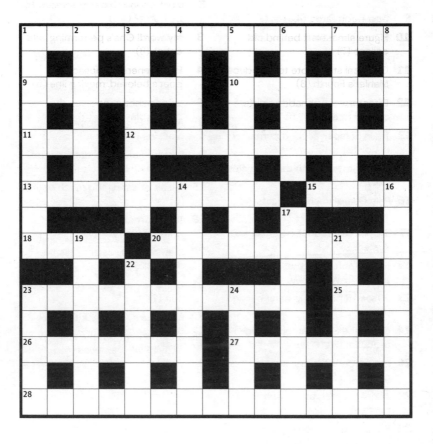

ACROSS

1 Value from Top Shop in roadside area (3,5,5,2)

9 Global struggle: virus from the east not treated (4,3)

10 Figure almost left behind old college (7)

11 Classical star's note to introduce Mahler's Fourth (3)

12 Directory of wannabe knights scared to fight? (6,5)

13 Falafel bits, eg nice round sandwiches fit to eat (10)

15 Thought Picaroon gives people a hand, briefly (4)

18 Losing heart, one's ridden the tube (4)

20 Cracking nut, a scarce thing with a shell? (10)

23 Made it with rice cooked for so long (11)

25 Hum opening of television program (3)

26 Old Indian copper seizing figure's sensitive appendage (7)

27 One wool-gathering artist reversed gauzy clothes (7)

28 I favour sweet, absorbing songs making lover's lament (1,2,8,4)

DOWN

1 Bit of a shock, economist's solution to key problem (9)

2 Winter food that's supposed to be burnt? (4,3)

3 My word! One's performing wild antics (8)

4 For listeners, Francesco the poet's beloved, moving line (5)

5 Having shot hoops, see the French playmaker (9)

6 Love kiss with these? They may be in bed (6)

7 Desperate need to consume crack, heading for altar (7)

8 Americans releasing article about old age (5)

14 Brilliant raid with train that's in motion (9)

16 Naked relative admitting a rule's broken (2,7)

17 Tablet's taken out of fatigue, showing caution (8)

19 Problem eating pastry up in a layer (7)

21 Ban poetic entreaty to hold me back (7)

22 Maybe two, four, six and zero still (4,2)

23 Rug with top-class exterior is an expensive fiddle (5)

24 Increased amount of liquor is enjoyed (5)

Solution see page 284

Set by Brendan

ACROSS

9 Excited cry from oaf (5)

10 I go off pastry sent around by a restaurant (9)

11 Herbivore long ago sorted out grasses, mostly (9)

12 Officers soundly managed area of woodland (5)

13 Visionary returns from hearing (7)

15 Shows emotion and is destructive? Doesn't sound like it (5,2)

17 Despotic leader installed without a break (5)

18 Role in Henry V sounds like something anyone could play (3)

20 Ruse that helps player secure contract (5)

22 See 3

25 Help with 24, a couple of 3 23 (7)

26 Audibly complaint increased in volume (5)

27 Legal agreements for shrinks (9)

30 Problem for driver scrambling to reverse (9)

31 Kind of love that's very open, like 8 and 15 exemplifying 3 7 (5)

DOWN

1 One or more positive responses viewers stated (4)

2 Forcibly removed — it's all over, one might say (5,3)

3,22 Term implying wisdom that's peculiarly man's? I hope so (4,7)

4 Put under financial pressure, stop being crooked, we hear (8)

5 Sign of something extra, or amount of gold, announced as incentive (6)

6 Being governed by chance upset constituents of a Scottish Conservative (10)

7 Plots to use G sharp in new composition (6)

8 China's tea with pronounced difference (4)

13 Diarist has a furtive look, reportedly (5)

14 Letters he has put in post to North and South? It's left, if not right (10)

16 Fire controller for game (5)

19 Male is awfully randy, resulting in this? (8)

21 Mocking boy, one I expelled, that's heavily protected (8)

23 In triumph, one smashes cells, perhaps (6)

24 Shoot, with 26, a pair of 3 23 (6)

26 Closing gap, don't stop thug (4)

28 As example of 3 18, raise back part ... (4)

29 ... or put an end to movement out of control (4)

Solution see page 285

110 Set by Paul

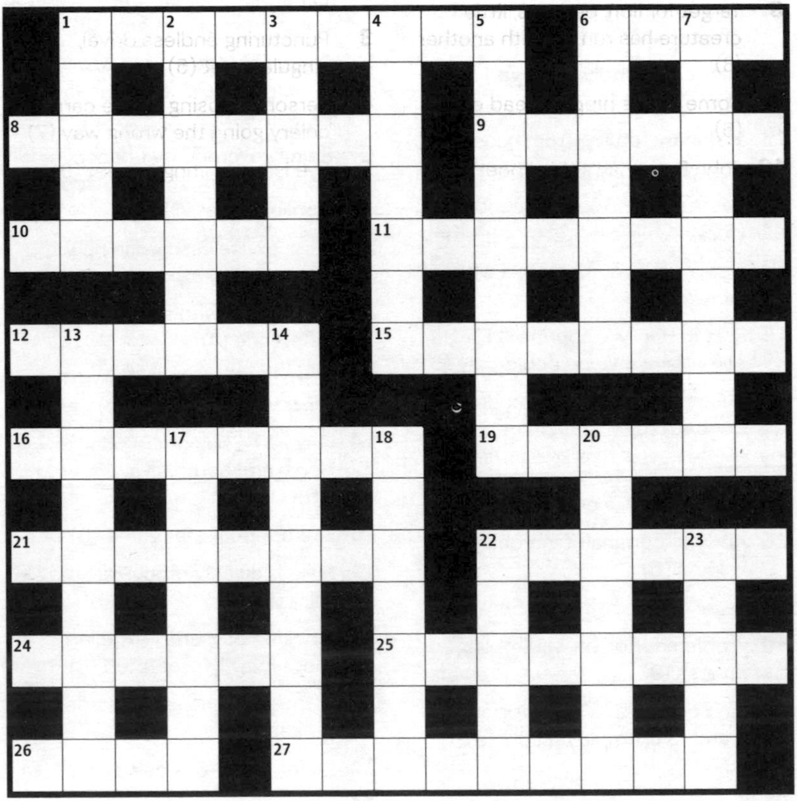

ACROSS

1 Poet feeding rats to damsel in distress (9)

6 3 reciting poem? (4)

8 Target for lion, perhaps, little creature has run off with another (8)

9 Some words nippers read out? (6)

10 John Betjeman's third poet recalled (6)

11 Agree to protect tease — in the family way? (8)

12 Work late? Male hasn't finished, certainly (4,2)

15 Poet ready to break Swiss dish (8)

16 Direction taken by writer in contribution to discussion? (8)

19 Bum touring new French city (6)

21 A new rake in motion, stir again (8)

22 Remain with server in shop (6)

24 Poet, Tennyson's subject under discussion? (6)

25 Poet in denial reviewing retrospective (8)

26 Issue: point overturned (4)

27 Demanding different results, serious failings initially concealed (9)

DOWN

1 Poet in squalor, number coming up (5)

2 Book Scottish island up for poet (7)

3 Puncturing endless drivel, singular poet (5)

4 Person choosing a little carrot, celery going the wrong way (7)

5 Eye issue limiting in poet (9)

6 Local interest in airline a monarch set up (4,3)

7 Paul's locked in 10s unfortunately — seasonal hang-up? (9)

13 Whistler carried by doddery mother out of that place (9)

14 Birds hearing poet who jumps from planes? (9)

17 Novel closer for poet (7)

18 After U-turn, minister working well in house (7)

20 Absolutely ludicrously hot inside pastry that's flipped over (3,4)

22 Poet takes Browning too far? (5)

23 Classic year incomplete, end of April void (5)

Solution see page 285

ACROSS

7 Odd job man gives fine performance with old tailless mongrel going head over heels (8)

9 Star carrying animal to old Japanese dictator (6)

10 Light close to central current unit (4)

11 Late MP ran frantically round independent part of government (10)

12 Introduction to timely subject in paper? (6)

14 Stand in part of theatre, including nationally acclaimed trio, initially (8)

15 Join priest cutting piece of cake? (6)

17 Man succeeding retired queen as interim ruler (6)

20 Do remote changes to measuring device (8)

22 Hand over vessel with metal coating (4,2)

23 Cleaner hid broken light (10)

24 See 2

25 One-dimensional retro part of transport infrastructure crossing small space (6)

26 Metal cask German sent abroad (8)

DOWN

1 A grave is disturbed causing unexpected changes (8)

2,24across Valve in vessels raised angle (8)

3 Basic recycled plates (6)

4 Judge has teatime altered to accommodate beginning of sentencing (8)

5 Comrade mixes with men, as appropriate (10)

6 Boat detailed to get container for fruit (6)

8 Surly animal crossing river (6)

13 Chap tucked into dish, then returned soldier's portable grill (10)

16 Animal heard about 22 down (8)

18 Check for second time in social media platform for one watching birds (8)

19 Performer in part is terrific (6)

21 Writer given one American plant (6)

22 Bishop's seat moved north-east (6)

24 Get rid of slight squint (4)

Solution see page 285

ACROSS

7 Fen country wife has dental treatment? (7)

8 Smelly lout overturned chest of drawers, US fashion (7)

9 Opposed to work's quality rating (4)

10 Rash move to open up someone local shot by an amateur? (4,5)

12 Rocker taking lead in Chicago, the musical? (5)

13 In which a monarch hid his approval to imprison one? (5,3)

15 Transported bird of prey — no alternative (4)

16 Figure submitted an account over the phone (5)

17 Debut of Gordon Fish, the writer (4)

18 'Seat of Government': article by ex-party leader (3,5)

20 Boxer's punch that shows something's wrong (5)

21 One of a poetic host's urns is cast almost sloppily (9)

22 Spirit needed by animal trainer (4)

24 Censoring device forced rebel to suppress past record (7)

25 A cold calm way to disappear? (7)

DOWN

1 Stupid people lacking college educator for ABC etc (4)

2 The panel rudely ignored occupant of room? (8)

3 A new job not quite providing security (6)

4 Passed round edible tubers wrong way up and caused alarm (8)

5 Implement obtained from second squalid home (6)

6 Old comedian's dance, ending in glide (4)

11 Ration one's expressions of appreciation when abroad? That'sbarbarous! (9)

12 Greyhound, maybe, in care of a church (5)

14 High spot, like going round Windy End (5)

16 Player gets sack — supporter takes a pee (8)

17 Look into playing for money after sunset (8)

19 Gym equipment bays (6)

20 Rook — mouldy thing with loathsome wings (6)

21 New start for fool, having no legal standing (4)

23 Sentimentality? Head off for boozer! (4)

Solution see page 286

ACROSS

1 Jump onto coach after morning with husband (6)

5 'Lost', say — a cult TV series (8)

9 Ambitious poisoner managed to inject it (8)

10 Secondary selection of vehicles serviced (6)

11 A few players romp back to the start (4)

12 Awfully primitive nurses roughly following Florence's lead (10)

13 Compound very like another is more unstable (6)

14 Escort to dungeon, perhaps, for final confrontation (8)

16 Dumpier person in illicit occupation (8)

19 Hamlet's last run in southern resort progressed well (6)

21 Leader staging demonstration on the coast (1,9)

23 Inspiration needed as European problem returns (4)

24 In moody period, king prowls around (6)

25 'Go over' means drivers can't stop here (8)

26 I proclaimed borders of country a beautiful sight (3,5)

27 Lower demand to hold sports training in recession (6)

DOWN

2 Woman being kept alive disheartened lofty Windsor resident (8,7)

3 Regular place to study protocol (7)

4 Two leaders meeting hastily (9)

5 Wench first to spurn sailor's arm (7)

6 Preserves workers on board (5)

7 Bore took it (7)

8 English dons that love Wilde's fanciful novel of Victorian life (3,3,5,4)

15 New parts where Riviera is improving (2,3,4)

17 Virtuous person funding play since regulars dropped out (7)

18 Lusty Romeo set off, losing head close to balcony (7)

20 Shame troops seizing southern capital in rebellion (7)

22 Artist depicted backward native, causing offence (5)

Solution see page 286

Set by Picaroon

ACROSS

1 Spin around and arouse cad after taking stimulants (4,2,4,4)

8 Deny King Edward, say, is making a comeback (5)

9 Very fat figure turns and runs before sumo wrestling (8)

11 Sell uniform seen in battle (7)

12 National football team containing king's back (7)

13 Record about holding vote for a leaver? (5)

15 Postal delivery of tea gets protection (5,4)

17 Post news, a conclusive piece (9)

20 Note on offbeat (5)

21 A slice of decent avocado in a little bread (7)

23 Asian drama work not a likely failure (2–5)

25 Vehicle left key English ring (9)

26 Parisian's bed? Out of it is out of it (3,2)

27 Liking corn mashed up isn't English attitude (14)

DOWN

1 Condiment a little Italian restaurant served up touching lip (7,5)

2 Something played live in playing field (5)

3 Reveal more attractive clothes come from here (9)

4 Marine's cocaine supply (7)

5 Tchaikovsky's First Symphony covers exciting material (7)

6 Poet in residence reading or writing? (5)

7 Jolly old soldier, say, catching cab (9)

10 One pound raised during life's works in this list (12)

14 Big cheese spread including old wine (9)

16 Love of the new mobile phone I trouble to bring back (9)

18 Work on huge problem for marsupial (7)

19 Waste long period of time in US prison (7)

22 Dispense nothing that's beyond Malachi? (5)

24 Stroke face of innocent chubby little children (5)

Solution see page 286

Set by Imogen

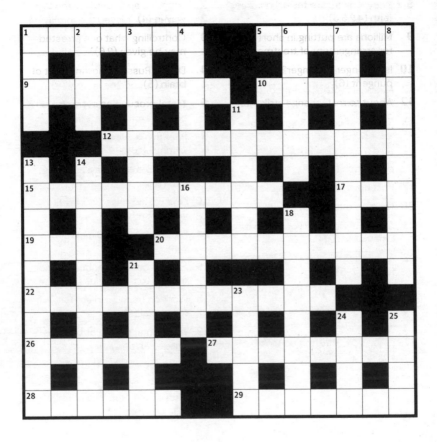

ACROSS

1 Looking offended by power trip (7)

5,26 Purported cure tested her good faith (4,2,3,3)

9 Millions are putting in short order for arrangement of treatment (8)

10 Is no longer a swinger? That's pungent (6)

12 About to rest, change striker for amateur game (7,5)

15 All you need to know about love: it's devastating and is huge (6,4)

17 Fool that a pedant picks (3)

19 Back page of The Dandy (3)

20 Cutting some potatoes set out in cold winds (10)

22 Endless capital employed by minister a bonus as betting is over (4,2,2,4)

26 See 5

27 Architect's trade vehicle, brown and horrible (8)

28 Comedian takes extremely large piece of cake (6)

29 Cut layer, about a yard — how much do you want? (3,4)

DOWN

1 Display anti-aircraft gun, ignoring one order (4)

2 Tongue bends double, finding way in (4)

3 Controlling what one arrested may be given (2,6)

4 Dodgy Russian showing a bit of brain (5)

6 Metal prostheses set these off? (6)

7 In which one can winningly play to the gallery (4,6)

8 Left tights off for check-up (6,4)

11 Hard villains finally cheated in hearing (6)

13 Bored, virtually carry out an unruly youth (10)

14 Get school to raise girl's death (10)

16 Look meaningfully round very fast (6)

18 Perhaps good in a sport, showing skill (8)

21 Expecting data, not quite everything (2,4)

23 Mountains of nettles picked up (5)

24 Pity it only has 4 chapters (4)

25 Flimsy item falling short (4)

Solution see page 287

ACROSS

1 Prince Andrew's regularly going out after sex, primarily in suit (6)

5 Depress actors by not working (4,4)

9 Token of love: attraction can feature? (4,4)

10 Go on run and walk (6)

11 Change her nappies with no dread (12)

13 Drop toast, essentially across floor? On the contrary (4)

14 Unusual tempo to maintain one piece of music (4,4)

17 One sticks with Tramp crossword, initially about to submit (8)

18 Rip short hem to denim outfit (4)

20 Number two fault: check by pilot (4–8)

23 Downed one can at end of month (8)

24 One might be smiling, feeling cold inside (8)

25 Avoids past graduates (8)

26 Case in hospital not so young (6)

DOWN

2 Secretary at work is smart? (4)

3 Stroke pet on top of paw and go off (3,6)

4 Shape second album during split (6)

5 Cherished ones lose footing away from Strictly Come Dancing (10,5)

6 See 12

7 Tips Democrat: American to limit Mike Pence (5)

8 Meow and start to enjoy cat milk, regularly put out: it's placed by front door (7,3)

12, 6 Criminal mostly and ten guys: Reservoir Dogs might see them? (10,8)

15 Sort out toilet pan: promise? (9)

16 What have you put on top of stuff that's not opened? Artwork? (9)

19 Way to get height to pass over low plane (6)

21 Another kiss? Tense during important date (5)

22 Drink and drugs (4)

Solution see page 287

ACROSS

8 They roared with wind by two but were swinging by three! (8)

9 Bathroom fitting is more splashy when I get in (6)

10 Apprentice never tried out leads for setter (4)

11 Obey Lorna, perhaps, by revising study ... (2,4,4)

12 ... recently put back in metal folder (2,4)

14 Philosopher abandoning case makes a cry for help (8)

15 Foremost Irish girl gets discharge, when rejected (7)

17 Impractical for campuses to become temporary shelters? (7)

20 A Swedish group has poetic scheme for this Lear favourite (8)

22 Aristocrat without a scrap found outside city (6)

23 Masons may roll it up to reveal support (7,3)

24 It comes early for one being sent off (4)

25 Standard element of animation plot (6)

26 After signal, shout 'open' (8)

DOWN

1 Disease picked up when the impossible happened (5,3)

2 Found out concealing key to correcting erroneous input (4)

3 Core position of hospital in NHS (6)

4 Champion finds partner online? (7)

5 US stock market regulator head promoted under European principles (8)

6 Unexpected visitor in winter trying to sell you something? (4,6)

7 Resolution satisfied ownership of property after it is abandoned (6)

13 Unreal chef cooked something that's supposedly never available (1,4,5)

16 Modest men daily get abused (8)

18 Broke unit revealing shade on the outside (4,4)

19 Almost miss promotion that could help ascending the slippery slope (3,4)

21 Cast-iron commercial progress (6)

22 He holds the money when company meets in bar (6)

24 Time attempt to capture rook (4)

Solution see page 287

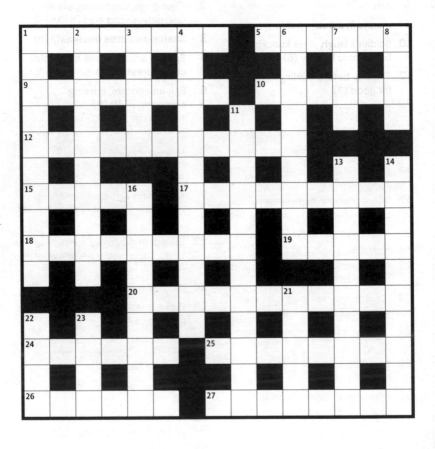

ACROSS

1 Topless dance after separation is out of sentimentality (8)

5 See 23

9 Marine in actual trouble (8)

10 Soldier's laugh, after knocking back some bubbly (6)

12 The day before starling went off for good (11)

15 Early form of atrioventricular valve (5)

17 Awkward question about a set of mathematical processes (9)

18 Tense situation for Britain in turmoil around April 5th and September 5th (9)

19 'County sees otherwise' (Times) (5)

20 Dish 2 as our little creation (11)

24 Bother to reject immorality for God (6)

25 Object to Spooner's Le Pétomane show? (8)

26 Laze about in empty Australia bush (6)

27 In status quo, talks about hostilities ending helped (8)

DOWN

1 Going down, lands in northern city (10)

2 Encourage to go outdoors? He's out, playing and wet! (5-5)

3 Sharon as a little mermaid? (5)

4 Special artist's event for an old cross-dresser (12)

6 Egg en cocotte, missing company, in 20 (9)

7,8 – a lockdown restaurant offering? (8)

11 The sound of tongues wagging: Orestes losing last couple of offies (6,6)

13 Unusual case taken by loyal advisor (10)

14 A male or female court, getting in deep, perhaps not surprising (2,8)

16 Goldberg with fiancé regularly in 20 (9)

21 Here little ones develop in computerisation (5)

22 How's it going for Champagne and sparkling wine? (4)

23,5 Latin clue for a stoic found in this province (4,6)

Solution see page 288

119 Set by Pasquale

ACROSS

4 Old-style language in new daily newspaper's leader (6)

6 Priest so funny making snappy replies? (8)

9 Merry Parisian is diving into English river (6)

10 Russians heading off with Europeans (8)

11 Unscrupulous man shows degree of speed, wanting evil woman back (11)

15 Fighter of old in hospital housing ethnic group (7)

17 Betray guerrilla fighter, then almost make amends (5,2)

18 Require alteration to top line in decorative work (11)

22 Plant to get fossil fuel reportedly? Not entirely raving mad (8)

23 Shine in speech? Modesty perhaps evident (6)

24 Record library with content written out in great detail (8)

25 Annoyed being listened to secretly (6)

DOWN

1 One cold dish served up with bread in the Gambia (6)

2 Bad local I repeatedly slammed as hellish (10)

3 Stories about wet girl (8)

4 Like extreme radical — maybe had biggest estate at death? (8)

5 Street vehicle in task removing what is grotty, ultimately? (8)

7 Bird leaves lake (4)

8 Realise social security covers America (4)

12 US financier set up — keeps playing a blinder (10)

13 Spectacular action of disenchanted workers (8)

14 Last thing park wants — no running water for plant (8)

16 Remorseful prisoner — first one in the religious ceremony (8)

19 Stop going up and down (4,2)

20 Glide or dash off, not finishing (4)

21 Avoid newspaper offered around hotel (4)

Solution see page 288

Set by Maskarade

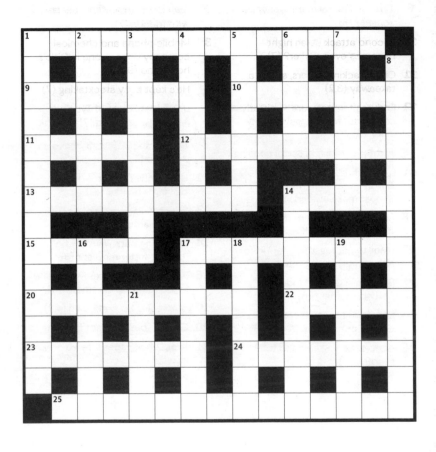

ACROSS

1 Little lad, one flogging camera? (14)

9 Wild garlic from butts above square (7)

10 Second attack when night becomes even darker? (7)

11 Chairs lacking covers, so get a takeaway (3,2)

12 Endures temperature — bitterly cold — at breaking point (4,5)

13 Seen on TV, they provide details of Ashes scores (4,5)

14 Dandy that's experienced at sea (5)

15 Sources of Riesling in Oppenheim — just any wine? (5)

17 Wind power in green area creating red tape (9)

20 Awkward matter with sexy Charlotte? (3,6)

22 Mondrian and a painting of the BVM (5)

23 Go wild — aggro is terrifying inside (7)

24 Those bearing gifts to mother — encircled by pieces of eight (3,4)

25 Pastor encourages English weed (9,5)

DOWN

1 County choristers were discordant (14)

2 Patients or prisoners at home with friends (7)

3 Mobile phone and chemical company once — one in Dido's homeland (9)

4 He's kept busy stocktaking (7)

5 Unavoidable fate of Tyneside canteen, I gathered (7)

6 These shallow waters upset sailing boat (5)

7 Studio location of horror film with final bits cut (7)

8 Book a week in it, local resort (1,4,4,5)

14 Repository for wrecked car (rear end missing), perhaps (9)

16 East German's wealthy bird (7)

17 Publicity broadcast that is plain (7)

18 Marked on the map, as the conspirator did (7)

19 Outdoor work — drop of early rain affected (4,3)

21 Dominant leg-spinner (2,3)

Solution see page 288

SOLUTIONS

1

```
W   L   H   A   B   J   S
MINOTAUR   EXACT
S   T   G   R   D   C   O
NETS   GRASSSKIRT
A   I   N   T   R   E
SCORES   GARLANDS
R   E   E   A   B
GETONES   OWNBACK
R   X   R   I   O
SANGUINE   SETTLE
T   A   G   V   I   A
CHANGELESS   SINK
O   I   N   K   E   D
MUSIC   GRIMACED
E   E   Y   E   N   T   R
```

2

```
F   L   A   V   O   U   R   O   F   T   H   E
B   E   N   B   A   I   O
OBLATES   COLOMBO
T   I   E   E   C   E   B
TOPDOGS   SCHERZI
O   E   C   S   E   U   T
MONTH   INCIDENCE
D   O   L   R
RURITANIA   EFFED
A   E   R   S   S   O   I
WASHOUT   SATYRIC
E   T   D   I   I   U   B   T
RWANDAN   CHATEAU
G   E   E   A   R   A   M
TENNISPLAYER
```

3

```
KNOWING   COWBOY
E   I   O   N   I   L   N
MOWN   SHELLSUITS
L   C   H   E   R   S   H
CICERO   DRIPFEED
T   W   L   G   O   G
THEMASSES   KUDOS
A   S   R
VANYA   OSTENSIVE
M   A   S   T   A   E
FALSETTO   ROSARY
D   W   R   S   L   A   S
HEREDITARY   BRIG
U   L   F   Y   O   L   O
PSALTER   INFERNO
```

SOLUTIONS

4

```
PAGANINI  BRIDGE
 H   R  N  M  O  N   R
MADOFF  PAWNSHOP
  M  A  O  S  E  U
CONARTIST  STING
 N   U   T   R  T  D
 TARTAR  COZENS
 H   E  T     Y  R  W
 ETCHER  LASSIE
 F   O  D  S  L    L
VIOLA  STRAWPOLL
 D   L  M  A   S  O
EDGETOOL  CANAPE
 L   C  R   A  O  Z  E
SEXTON  GSTRINGS
```

5

```
  GREASYSPOON
P  O  X  T  O  P   I  C
HILLIER  BEEFTEA
Y  D  S  E  E   N  R  L
SPECTATOR  FROZE
I  N    T   U  I  G  N
OOPS  COPPERHEAD
T  A  F     E   N  A
HOROLOGIST  ODOR
E  A  E  R  C    I  G
ROCKS  AFORTIORI
A  H  H  N  R  E  X  R
PLUMPED  PARTIAL
Y  T  O  P  I  R  D  S
  EXTRAPOLATE
```

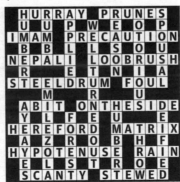

6

```
 HURRAY  PRUNES
 U  U  P  W  E  O  P
IMAM  PRECAUTION
 B  B  L  L  S  O  U
NEPALI  LOOBRUSH
 R   E  T  N  I  A
STEELDRUM  FOUL
    M    R    U
 ABIT  ONTHESIDE
 Y  L  F  E  U    E
HEREFORD  MATRIX
 A  Z  R  O  B  H  F
HYPOTENUSE  RAIN
 E  L  S  T  R  O  E
 SCANTY  STEWED
```

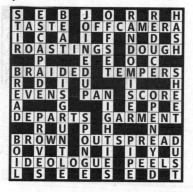

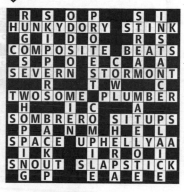

SOLUTIONS

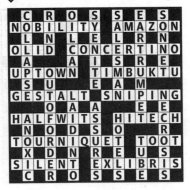

10

```
C R O S S E S       S
NOBILITY       AMAZON
L   N   L   E   L R   N
OLID   CONCERTINO
A     A   I   S R   E
UPTOWN   TIMBUKTU
S   U       E   A M
GESTALT   SNIPING
  O   A   A       E   E
HALFWITS   HITECH
N   O   D   S O       R
TOURNIQUET   TOOT
X   D   N   R   E   U S
SILENT   EXLIBRIS
  C   R   O   S S E S
```

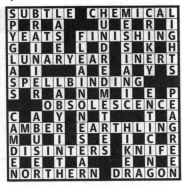

11

```
SUBTLE   CHEMICAL
P   R   A       U E R   I
YEATS   FINISHING
G   I   E   L   D   S K   H
LUNARYEAR   INERT
A   I       A E   A Y   S
SPELLBINDING
S   R   A N   M I E   P
    OBSOLESCENCE
C   A   Y N   T       T A
AMBER   EARTHLING
M   U   I   S   E   I C   R
DISINTERS   KNIFE
E   E   T   A       E N   E
NORTHERN   DRAGON
```

12

```
    PRESSGANGED
V U C   A   D   R R   B
OUTFLOW   ARABICA
L   T   A D   P F V   R
UNITTRUST   FLEET
M   N       S E   I N   O
ERGO   STARSTRUCK
    T   F       I   P
DOODLEBUGS   STAB
O   G   O   A R       H E
CHEAT   STOCKIEST
K   T   I E   W I   W R
ECHELON   BANDANA
T   E L   J   A   D L   Y
    READINGGAOL
```

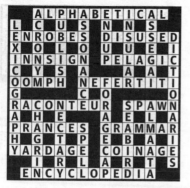

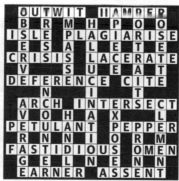

SOLUTIONS

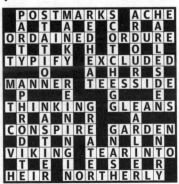

19

```
C T S     D   A   F
B A H R A I N   B O U R B O N
V I L     M   T   R
H A I L   V A R N I S H E D
  L   E   E   N   U
F L I E R   F O O T R A C E
I   A     R   E       A
O V E N   A D A M S   D E N T
E     M C     O   A
C R A B M E A T   H A Z E L
  I   T O     E
M E G A H E R T Z   D U D E
A   W   Y     A   O   U
T R A I P S E   P R E F E C T
Y   G T     D   F   K
```

20

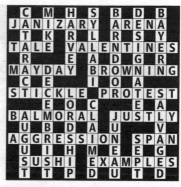

```
C M H S   B D   B
J A N I Z A R Y   A R E N A
T K R L   R S   Y
T A L E   V A L E N T I N E S
R   E   A D G   R
M A Y D A Y   B R O W N I N G
C E   I O   A
S T I C K L E   P R O T E S T
E O C     E A
B A L M O R A L   J U S T L Y
U B D   A U   V
A G G R E S S I O N   S P A N
U I H   M E   E G
S U S H I   E X A M P L E S
T T P   D U   T D
```

21

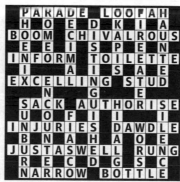

```
P A R A D E   L O O F A H
H O   E D K   I   A
B O O M   C H I V A L R O U S
E E   I   S P   E   N
I N F O R M   T O I L E T T E
I   A   I S   A   E
E X C E L L I N G   S T U D
  N   G     E
S A C K   A U T H O R I S E
U O   F I   I   I
I N J U R I E S   D A W D L E
B N   A H   A   O   E
J U S T A S W E L L   R U N G
R E   C D   G   S   C
N A R R O W   B O T T L E
```

SOLUTIONS

22

```
FATHER  PISSARRO
V   A  E   U  A R  E
MIDNIGHT   YASMIN
 D  D  I    O  O   N
   SANGUINENESS
 A  D  A    T  A    T
AFRO    MOROCCAN
 I  W  D   O  A  H  T
SCANTIER    RUED
 I    R   E  A  I   S
COUNTERFEITS
 N  A  C   L  L  T   A
DAMMIT   ABITMUCH
 D  E  O   G  N  A  M
CONSORTS  GASKET
```

23

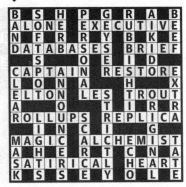

```
B  S  H  P G  R  A   B
ALONE  EXECUTIVE
N  F   R  R Y  B  K   E
DATABASES  BRIEF
  S     O   E  I  D
CAPTAIN  RESTORE
L   O   N  A   H     X
ELTON  LES  TROUT
A   O   A   T  I  R   R
ROLLUPS  REPLICA
  I   N  C  I   G
MAGIC  ALCHEMIST
A   H  E   R  T C  N  A
SATIRICAL  HEART
K   S   S  E   Y  O   E
```

24

```
  INDIANCLUBS
A  T  R  U O  N  H  A
DIAMOND  WEDDING
V  L  N  I  H  E  P  R
EPICENTRE  RHONE
R  A    O  R  A  F  E
TANG  PREDICATED
   V  C     T  H
ONEWAYTRIP  LESS
N  R  U  A N   D  P
CAMEL  BATHSHEBA
O  O   D  A  R  A S D
SQUIRMS  UKULELE
T   T  O  C  T  N  R  D
  HANDONHEART
```

25

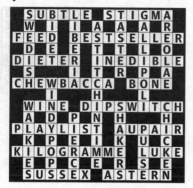

```
S U B T L E   S T I G M A
W   I   I   A   A   A   R
F E E D   B E S T S E L L E R
D   E   E   T   L   O
D I E T E R   I N E D I B L E
S   I   T   R   P   A
C H E W B A C C A   B O N E
    I   H   L
  W I N E   D I P S W I T C H
A   D   P   N   H   H
P L A Y L I S T   A U P A I R
K   P   E   I   K   U   C
K I L O G R A M M E   L U K E
E   P   C   E   R   S   E
S U S S E X   A S T E R N
```

26

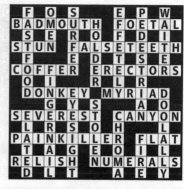

```
  F   O S       E   P   W
B A D M O U T H   F O E T A L
  S   E   R   O   F   D   I
S T U N   F A L S E T E E T H
  F       E   D   T   S   E
C O F F E R   E R E C T O R S
  O   I       R   L   R
  D O N K E Y   M Y R I A D
      G   Y S       A   O
S E V E R E S T   C A N Y O N
  L   R   S   O   H   L
P A I N K I L L E R   F L A T
  T   A   G   E   O   I L
R E L I S H   N U M E R A L S
  D   L   T       A   E Y
```

27

```
      M     C   R
D O C T O R   C H A R L O C K
I   A   R   A   E   P   I
A R R E S T   G R A D I E N T
S   D   E   L   A   N   E
P E A R L E S C E N T
O   M       T   S O D   S
R E O R D E R   T O R R E N T
A   M   O   O   O     S   R
    M A G I N O T L I N E
S   P   I   A   R   G   A
P O I G N A N T   M A G N U M
O   M   A   O   G   E   E
T I P S T A F F   M I R R O R
    E   F       C
```

SOLUTIONS

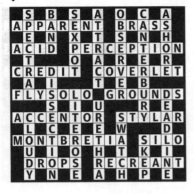

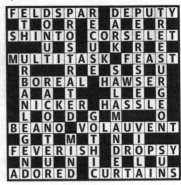

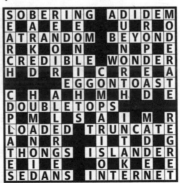

 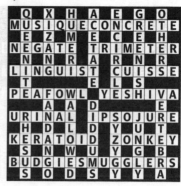

SOLUTIONS

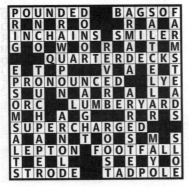

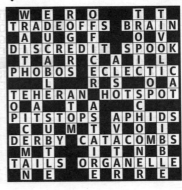

37

```
E D B M I D H D
DARKROOMS ERATO
I A E N O L B G
TIGER KITTIWAKE
O R E O N
FANTASY NEWYEAR
E B N I E R E
VOCAB SEC SNAKE
E H I T T V
ROOSTER CHINESE
I A L N P
HORSEHIDE DJINN
O M P G A I G U
OXEYE HAVEAGOAT
P N E T E N N S
```

38

```
PICADOR TUMBLED
O O I A A O I O
LORDS VANCOUVER
Y V E E G T E M O
POIGNANTLY BRIO
S D C E D I U S
HEADDRESSES
S A A I U M H E
MANONTROPPO
U O T P G F P
GORY LIPSERVICE
G E C R T A N P
LUXURIATE POINT
E I O C E H S I
ROADWAY PSYCHIC
```

39

```
M I D S C D
CALIGULA HERBAL
T M N G O E Y
FETA OPENTHEBOX
S U O N N
WHILST LOVELIER
I I D E I
PIGEON BRUGES
H V O H H
MONTREAL OBTAIN
N G R D U P
DEPRESSANT MEMO
D E H G R A A
GAZEBO EQUALITY
Y N T N I E
```

SOLUTIONS

40

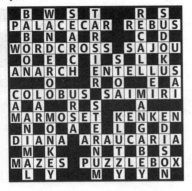

```
 B   W    S  T        R  S
PALACECAR    REBUS
 B   N    A  R    C   D
WORDCROSS    SAJOU
 O   E    I  S    L   K
ANARCH    ENTELLUS
     O    R  O    E   A
COLOBUS   SAIMIRI
 A   A    R  S    A
MARMOSET    KENKEN
 N   O    A  E    L   D
DIANA   ARAUCARIA
 M   K    N  T    B   S
MAZES   PUZZLEBOX
 L   Y    M  Y    Y   N
```

41

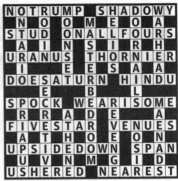

```
NOTRUMP  SHADOWY
 N   O   O   M  E  O  A
STUD  ONALLFOURS
 A   I   N   S  I  R  H
URANUS   THORNIER
 I   E   E   S  A  A
DOESATURN   HINDU
     E   B   L
SPOCK  WEARISOME
 R   R   A   D  E  A
FIVESTAR   VENUES
 A   T   H   O  E  O  N
UPSIDEDOWN   SPAN
 U   V   N   M  G  I  D
USHERED  NEAREST
```

42

```
 P   S  B  B  S  C  I  C
AFTERMATH    OOMPH
 S   O  I  B  O  M  P  I
SINEDIE    TAPERED
 M   E  L     P  A  O
UKASE   BOUNDOVER
 S   G  L  T  R     E
THEARTOFTHEDEAL
 E   E  O  E  X  I
REMAINDER   SOAVE
 A   N  Y     Q  C  F
POTSDAM   CHUNTER
 O   T  E  A  U  I  I  O
SUEDE   REFERENDA
 E   R  R  Y  F  E  G  D
```

43

 44

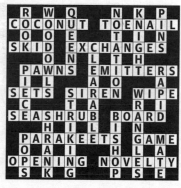

45

SOLUTIONS

46

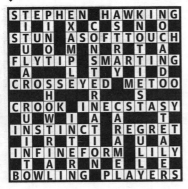

```
STEPHEN  HAWKING
 I   I X   C   S   N   O
STUN  ASOFTTOUCH
 U   O M   N R   T   A
FLYTIP   SMARTING
 A   L   T   Y   I D
CROSSEYED  METOO
 H   R   R      S
CROOK  INECSTASY
 U W   I   A   A   T
INSTINCT  REGRET
 I   R   T-I   U A
INFINEFORM   LILY
 T   A R   N   E   E
BOWLING  PLAYERS
```

47

```
DARKWEB  GNOSTIC
E  E   A   A O   V   E L
PIVOT  SULTANATE
I  A   E   I D   L   R A
COMPRESSED   AIRO
T  P   B      N   A W   F
   QUARTERSTAFF
M D   T E   Y   T   Y F
ABOUTTIMETOO
I  G   S   T   U   S O
NEW   ZEALANDERS
L  A   L   R O   D X   P
INTHEWARS  INTER
N  C   A   T   E   N O E
ENHANCE  REGENCY
```

48

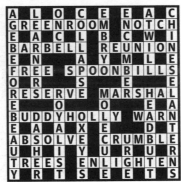

```
A   L O C E   E   A C
GREENROOM  NOTCH
E  A C   L   B C   W   I
BARBELL  REUNION
E  N   A   Y M   L E
FREE  SPOONBILLS
O  R   S   E   E
RESERVE  MARSHAL
E   O   O   E A
BUDDYHOLLY  WARN
E  A A   X   E D   T
ABSOLVE  CRUMBLE
U  H I   Y   U R   U R
TREES  ENLIGHTEN
Y  R T   S   E E   T S
```

SOLUTIONS

52

P	I	P	E	M	M	A		I	L	L	E	G	A	L
O		I	A	V		N		A	O		U			U
B	I	L	L	Y	G	O	A	T		S	T	U	M	P
O		L	A	G		H		S		R				I
X	I	A	N		G	A	M	E	W	A	R	D	E	N
		G	A	D		L		F		E				E
H	E	A	R	E	R		A	S	E	P	S	I	S	
		C		O		S		V						
A	G	O	U	T	I	S		T	E	E	O	F	F	
R		U	I	N		R		R		L				
C	A	T	E	C	H	U	M	E	N		D	I	E	S
H		R	T		M	S		M		C	T			
I	R	A	T	E		B	I	O	M	A	R	K	E	R
N		C	R	E		R		R		L	E			A
G	L	E	A	N	E	R		T	U	T	O	R	E	D

53

S		H	S		S	O		R		R		M
I	D	E	N	T	I	C	A	L		A	M	I	G	O
Z		T	A		A	D		N		C		B
E	M	E	R	Y		R	O	G	U	I	S	H	L	Y
		R	A	E		U				A		
S	P	O	T	T	E	D		A	D	M	I	R	E	R
O		H			R		E		D		A
L	O	T	T	O		C	I	D		C	A	S	T	S
I		R	M	R				H			P
D	E	A	D	E	Y	E		F	R	A	N	C	I	S
		C		S		I		N		R		
K	I	T	C	A	R	S	O	N		I	V	O	R	Y
I		I	H		I		I	C		W		O
N	I	O	B	E		D	A	S	T	A	R	D	L	Y
G		N	M		A		H		L		S			O

54

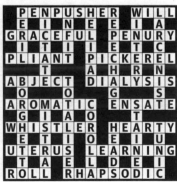

	P	E	N	P	U	S	H	E	R		W	I	L	L
	E		I		N	E		E		I		A		
G	R	A	C	E	F	U	L		P	E	N	U	R	Y
	I		T		I		I		E	T		C		
P	L	I	A	N	T		P	I	C	K	E	R	E	L
	T				A		H		R		N			
A	B	J	E	C	T		D	I	A	L	Y	S	I	S
	O		O				G			S				
A	R	O	M	A	T	I	C		E	N	S	A	T	E
	G		I		A	O			T					
W	H	I	S	T	L	E	R		H	E	A	R	T	Y
	E		T		I	O		E		I		U		
U	T	E	R	U	S		L	E	A	R	N	I	N	G
	T		A		E		L		D		E		I	
R	O	L	L		R	H	A	P	S	O	D	I	C

55

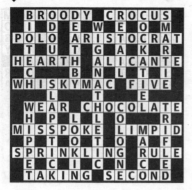

```
B R O O D Y   C R O C U S
I   D   E   W   E   O   M
P O L O   A R I S T O C R A T
T   U   T   G   A   K   R
H E A R T H   A L I C A N T E
C       B   N   L   T   I
W H I S K Y M A C   F I V E
    L   T       E
  W E A R   C H O C O L A T E
  H   P   L   L   O   R
M I S S P O K E   L I M P I D
P   T   O   T   O   A   F
S P R I N K L I N G   R U L E
E   C   I   C   N   C   E
  T A K I N G   S E C O N D
```

 56

```
L E G A C Y   S P R U C E U P
U   I   A   O   B   X   O
B R A I N S   E S T O P P E L
E   C   T   T   A   L   Y
  L O U I S A R M S T R O N G
  M   C   P   A   S   I   O
S P O I L S P O R T   S T U N
U   E   O   K   A   U
B A B Y   D I N I N G R O O M
G   I   O   N   N   A   I
E L L A F I T Z G E R A L D
N   L   F   M   A   I   I
E Y E L I N E R   A G R E E D
R   T   S   N   A   S   E
A E S T H E T E   B R U T U S
```

 57

```
H O L I D A Y   W H I S K E R
R   N   I   I   I   T   X
B I R D   R E A L T E N N I S
G   I   L   R   M   G   G
P A L A C E   A V E R A G E S
M   S   N   N   P   N
F I V E A S I D E   P O T T Y
  X   F       R
E L V E S   R E F E R E N C E
E   C   B   A   N   H
S C A R I E S T   F A S T E R
T   A   M   H O   P   M
A U C T I O N E E R   A X I S
R   E   A   R   C   I   S
V E R D A N T   P E A N U T S
```

SOLUTIONS

58

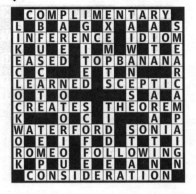

59

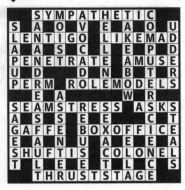

60

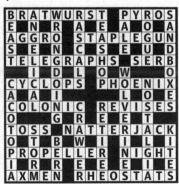

61

```
. D I S H T H E D I R T .
L . I . A . E X M . H . R
E P S I L O N . P O M P E I I
F . A . O D . U . A . P . G
T I P A N D R U N . T I L T H
W . P . . I . G . U . O . T
E V E N . A L L E G R E T T O
L . A . D . . . E . T . F .
L A R K A R O U N D . C H I C
A . I . Y . B . O . . I . E
L I N E D . L O R D L U C A N
O . G . R . A . T . O K . T
N E A R E S T . H A U T E U R
E . C . A . E . S . N . E
. T I M E S E R V E R S .
```

62

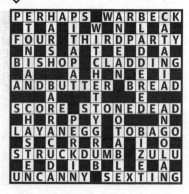

```
P E R H A P S . W A R B E C K
T . A . I . W N . L . A
F O U R . T H I R D P A R T Y
N . S . A . T . E . D . A
B I S H O P . C L A D D I N G
A . A . H . N . E . I
A N D B U T T E R . B R E A D
. A . . . T . . . E
S C O R E . S T O N E D E A D
H . R . P . Y . O . N
L A Y A N E G G . T O B A G O
S . C . R . R . A . I . O
S T R U C K D U M B . Z U L U
E . D . I . B . L . E . A
U N C A N N Y . S E X T I N G
```

63

```
B T N . M L . W C E
L A R G E . U N A B A S H E D
E I O . S . U . S . I . G
D O M I N I C A N . H A S T E
. A . A . C . I . E
W O R S T E D . H A N D L E S
A . A . R . E . G . . . C
R A N G E . T O P . T I G E R
D . N . O . O . A . E
S O L I C I T . W I N D R O W
. I . H . E . D . D
T O N I C . S P E E D W E L L
O . E . O . T . R . A . N O
M A N G A N E S E . C H I M P
E . S . T . S . D . E . A E
```

SOLUTIONS

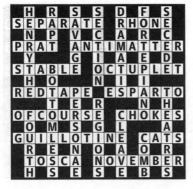

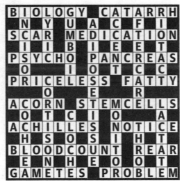

67

```
S A P P H O   T H E S I S
C   O   A   S   U   U   I
C H I P   P O P E M O B I L E
E   P   P   I B   W   V
A R G Y L E   K E E L O V E R
Z       N   E   R   O   R
D O N T A S K M E   I F F Y
    H       I   E
  S H O T   G L A M O R I S E
  T   U   A   L   O   E
M I S S O U R I   B H U T A N
R   A   S G S   M   R
C R A N K S H A F T   A S I T
U   D   I   N   E M   N
P O S T E R   I R V I N G
```

68

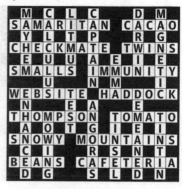

```
  M   C L   C     D   M
S A M A R I T A N   C A C A O
  Y   L   T   P     R   G
C H E C K M A T E   T W I N S
  E   U   U   A E   I   E
S M A L L S   I M M U N I T Y
    U       N   M       I
W E B S I T E   H A D D O C K
  N   E   A     E
T H O M P S O N   T O M A T O
  A   O   T   G   I   E   I
S N O W Y   M O U N T A I N S
  C   I       R   S   N   T
B E A N S   C A F E T E R I A
  D   G       S   L   D   N
```

69

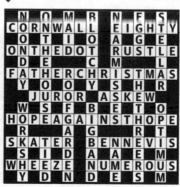

```
  N   O M   R     N   F   S
C O R N W A L L   E I G H T Y
  O   T   I   O   A   G   E
O N T H E D O T   R U S T L E
  D   E   C   M       L
F A T H E R C H R I S T M A S
  Y   O   O Y   S   H   R
    J U R O R   A S K E W
  W   S F   B   E   T   O
H O P E A G A I N S T H O P E
  R   A   G     R   T
S K A T E R   B E N N E V I S
  S   I   D   A   A   E   M
W H E E Z E   N U M E R O U S
  Y   D N   D   E   S   M
```

SOLUTIONS

Grid 70:

```
E S C B F C W   O
METRONOME ONAIR
I R A I L M T B
TROUT LOOSENESS
  B H E N   R
BEEFAND ORACLES
  L N U L O T
UNPEG SOS GLOVE
E E E H   O P
SETFREE CARROTS
  A B O I V
BANDSTAND TIERS
U Q I N D H R O
MOUND GOLDMEDAL
P E E S E S O O
```

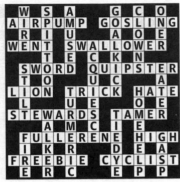

Grid 71:

```
W S A   G C O
AIRPUMP GOSLING
R I U A O E
WENT SWALLOWER
T E C K N
SWORD QUIPSTER
T O U C A
LION TRICK HATE
L U E O E
STEWARDS TAMER
A M C I E
FULLERENE HIGH
I K R D E A
FREEBIE CYCLIST
E R C E P P
```

Grid 72:

```
INDEPTH MONOPOD
N A L A I E A E
FAMOUSLASTWORDS
O E T L S E T I
CELLO EXHORTING
U A C A C N
SQUAREDUP TALUS
R A I E A E
MEANT SANDPIPER
A K T E H E
WINEGLASS DRYUP
K I L N Y R S I
INGOODCONDITION
S H B E O V C E
HATLESS DRESSED
```

272

73

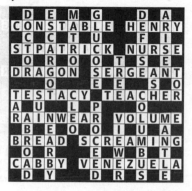

```
D E M G     D A
C O N S T A B L E   H E N R Y
C C T U   F I
S T P A T R I C K   N U R S E
O R O O T S E
D R A G O N   S E R G E A N T
O E E S O
T E S T A C Y   T E A C H E R
A U L P O
R A I N W E A R   V O L U M E
B E O O I U A
B R E A D   S C R E A M I N G
O R E W B T
C A B B Y   V E N E Z U E L A
D Y D R S E
```

74

```
C M M T O S Q
M A R A D O N A   P R I M U S
S N Z C E G A
R A C Y   A F T E R S H A V E
N R I A T E
C O R S E T   L I T E R A R Y
V H E I E
T A V E N E R   S C R A T C H
E N A D O
S T I T C H E D   R E S U L T
W M E D A D
S E C U L A R I S M   B E S T
N S R C E A O
S T R I P S   T R A M C A R S
Y C E S U H E
```

75

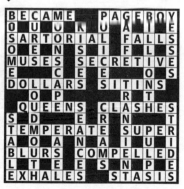

```
B E C A M E   P A G E B O Y
O U U N A E
S A R T O R I A L   F A L L S
O E N S I F L S
M U S E S   S E C R E T I V E
E C E E O S
D O L L A R S   S I T I N S
O P R T
  Q U E E N S   C L A S H E S
S D E R N T
T E M P E R A T E   S U P E R
A O A N A I U I
B L U R S   C O M P E L L E D
L T E E S N P E
E X H A L E S   S T A S I S
```

SOLUTIONS

76

```
CONGAME MERCURY
V O A C N A A
SELF GHOSTTRAIN
R A E N A D S
FLORIN THISISIT
A T R L N N
EYESHADOW MANGO
P V L
SPLAT DENTISTRY
L D A R U E
PAGEANTS NERUDA
C W G I U W
NEWORLEANS BAIT
B R E L I I N
ROCKERY YANKEES
```

77

```
E S V R A A C A
PROSEPOEM DYLAN
I N R N I A E O
CANTS DECAMERON
E E E A I
HATEFUL BATCHED
A O L R E I
IDLER ODE ATWAR
K I M B N G
UNMASKS AUSTERE
E S T L I N
FIREALARM SEVER
I I B C O T O I
JACOB LONDONISM
I K A E D R S E
```

78

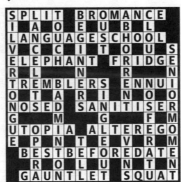

```
SPLIT BROMANCE
I A O E U B L
LANGUAGESCHOOL
V C C I T O U S
ELEPHANT FRIDGE
R L N R R N
TREMBLERS ENNUI
O T A R I N O O
NOSED SANITISER
G M G F M
UTOPIA ALTEREGO
E P N T E V R M
BESTBEFOREDATE
R O L U N T N
GAUNTLET SQUAT
```

79

```
C O S T A R S   L A R G I S H
O   E   P   P   I   I   D   E
R A D I O   A R G E N T I N A
O   A   S   C   H   G   O   V
N I N E T E E N T H   C L U E N
A   S   A   E   E   E   N
    A S T R O N O M I C A L
N   A   I   E   U   E   T   Y
E X T R E M E S P O R T
B   T   S   N       A   C   B
U S E D   Z A B A G L I O N E
L   N   D   C   G   D   S   L
O L D M A S T E R   C O M E T
U   E   H   O   E   U   I   E
S T E L L A R   E N T I C E D
```

80

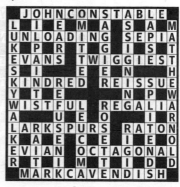

```
  J O H N C O N S T A B L E
L   I   E   M   A   S A   M
U N L O A D I N G   S E P I A
K   P   R   T   G   I   S T
E V A N S   T W I G G I E S T
S   I   E   E       N   H
K I N D R E D   R E I S S U E
Y   T   E       N   P   W
W I S T F U L   R E G A L I A
A   U   E   O   I
L A R K S P U R S   R A T O N
K   A   E   C   E   I   O
E V I A N   O C T A G O N A L
R   T   M   T   I   D   D
M A R K C A V E N D I S H
```

81

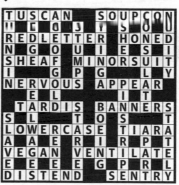

```
T U S C A N   S O U P C O N
U   E   O   J   S   O   U
R E D L E T T E R   H O N E D
N   G   O   U   I   E   S I
S H E A F   M I N O R S U I T
I   G   P   G   L   Y
N E R V O U S   A P P E A R
    E   L       I   T
  T A R D I S   B A N N E R S
S   L   T   O   S   T
L O W E R C A S E   T I A R A
A   A   E   R   I   R   P T
V E G A N   V E N T I L A T E
E   E   E   E   G   P R   L
D I S T E N D   S E N T R Y
```

SOLUTIONS

82

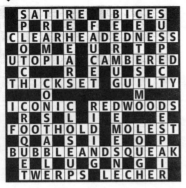

```
S A T I R E   I B I C E S
P   R   E   F   E   E   U
C L E A R H E A D E D N E S S
O   M   E   U   R   T   P
U T O P I A   C A M B E R E D
C   R   E   U   S   C
T H I C K S E T   G U I L T Y
    O               M
I C O N I C   R E D W O O D S
R   S   L   I   E   E
F O O T H O L D   M O L E S T
Q   A   S   I   E   O   P
B U B B L E A N D S Q U E A K
E   L   U   G   N   G   I
T W E R P S   L E C H E R
```

83

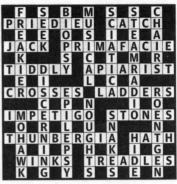

```
  F   S   B   M   S   S   C
P R I E D I E U   C A T C H
E   E   O   S   I   E   A
J A C K   P R I M A F A C I E
K   S   C   T   M   R
T I D D L Y   A P I A R I S T
E   I   L   C   A
C R O S S E S   L A D D E R S
  C   P   N   I   O
I M P E T I G O   S T O N E S
O   R   L   U   N   N
T H U N B E R G I A   H A T H
A   I   P   H   K   I   G
W I N K S   T R E A D L E S
K   G   Y   S   S   E   N
```

84

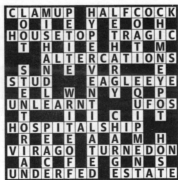

```
C L A M U P   H A L F C O C K
O   I   E   Y   E   O   H
H O U S E T O P   T R A G I C
T   H   I   E   H   T   M
    A L T E R C A T I O N S
S   N   E   V   R   E
S T U D   E A G L E E Y E
E   L   W   N   Y   Q   P
U N L E A R N T   U F O S
T   I   I   C   I   T
H O S P I T A L S H I P
R   E   E   A   A   M   H
V I R A G O   T U R N E D O N
A   C   F   E   G   N   S
U N D E R F E D   E S T A T E
```

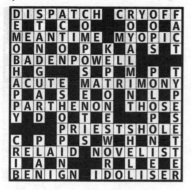 

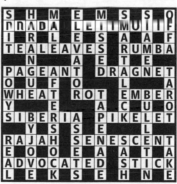

SOLUTIONS

88

```
V I A D U C T   R E M A I N S
E   C   T   R   I   I   R   T
S A I N T   A U G U S T I N E
P   D   E   N   I   M   S   R
E T H E R I S E D   A S H E N
R   O   M   N   N   L
S C U L L   I N A B A D W A Y
  S   A   T   N   G   O
F R E E M A S O N   E C L A T
U   I   A   A   F   U
C A P O N   C A L L A G H A N
H   A   A   A   I   T   O   E
S T R U T O N E S   S T U F F
I   T   E   A   T   E   N   U
A B Y S S A L   S C A N D A L
```

89

```
        B       P S
M A R G I N   M A J E S T I C
O   E   N   L   Q   R   U
T A M P E R   F A B U L I S T
I   S   N   T   I   P   E
V A L E D I C T I O N
A   E   O   N   E   F   T
T R E E T O P   A N D O R R A
E   P   R   P   T   E   X
    I L E D E F R A N C E
A   T   B   R   O   Z   X
B A R O U C H E   S O L I D I
U   E   N   E   T   E   L
T A K E A W A Y   B E A D L E
    L   D       D
```

90

```
B   B   D   E S   D   P   S
R E A R R A N G E   Y E A S T
E   C   O   V   C   S   L   Y
A U T O P S Y   O U T R A G E
S   E   S   N   O   T
T A R D Y   B E D S P R E A D
B   I   L   W   I   U
O R A L E X A M I N A T I O N
N   V   C   N   R   D
E A R M A R K E D   C H O K E
  E   C   B   R   N   R
D E N T U R E   S Q U E L C H
I   N   A   A   O   E   U   E
S W E A T   R U R I T A N I A
C   T   E   D   E S   G   D
```

91

```
  B A N D E R S N A T C H
B   I   A   S M   D   A   B
O W L E T   S N O W D O N I A
O   A   I   E   K   L   O   R
J O T D O W N   E L E M E N T
U   E   N   B   D       O
M O R T A L B L O W   P A R K
  A   L   O   M   F F
J I L L   J A B B E R W O C K
O   O   V   T   A   R   R
C A R R O L L   T A B L E A U
O   O   R   O   H   J   S   G
S O U P P L A T E   O R A T E
E   T   A   D   R   U   I   R
  W E L L A S S E S S E D
```

92

```
      L   B       S   E
S E E R E D   D E O D A R
  C   I   S   A   R G   E
W H Y N O T   P E A R I F L E
  L   S   O   P   P E   A
T E A T   W E A T H E R E Y E
  P   E     R   I       S
    C R Y P T I C C L U E
  R     A   T     N   A
S E A F I S H I N G   P A C Y
  A   I   T   O   L   O   T
E L E C T I O N   I B E R I A
  L   H   M   S   T   T   N
Y O U B E T   I C H I N G
    S   S       H   C
```

93

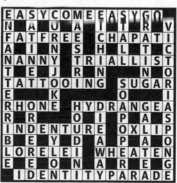

```
E A S Y C O M E E A S Y G O
N   A   U   A   T T   R   V
F A T F R E E   C H A P A T I
A   I   N   S   H   L   T   C
N A N N Y   T R I A L L I S T
T   E   J   R   N   N   O
T A T T O O I N G   S U G A R
E       K       O       R
R H O N E   H Y D R A N G E A
R   R   O   I   P   A   S
I N D E N T U R E   O X L I P
B   E   Y   D   A   P   A   O
L O R E L E I   W H E A T E N
E   E   O   N   A   R   E G
  I D E N T I T Y P A R A D E
```

SOLUTIONS

94

```
FLIPPED BUCKRAM
O N R A E O A O
GENRE LOGCABINS
L O Y A U L T E
ACCESSION FLAKY
M E L I E
PANTS AMPERSAND
C O M I E N
REENTRANT DROOP
E T C M O
PATIO BOHEMIANS
A I V E F I L S
IMBROGLIO SCORE
R I C A R D U S
STATELY KNOSSOS
```

95

```
RECOGNITION
P E O E A R E U
ROMULUS SCREWIN
O A I T K U S A
STIRCRAZY PACED
O N P O T O U
POST MONUMENTAL
A T A D L T
GROUSEMOOR FACE
N B S A E N R
OBESE ROUGHIDEA
S S N R V A Y T
INEPTLY RESHAPE
A E E I E T R D
NODONESHEAD
```

96

```
O B S C
JUNKER STRAFE
I T H M U S T
ANTIFA AUTOBAHN
X P L N T A N
FEST FAHRENHEIT
D O A R C
GERMANISING
C A D E S
ROTTWEILER ECHT
B R C I A D E
FRAULEIN KAISER
A M N G E E S
STALAG PUTSCH
N S P T
```

97

 98

 99

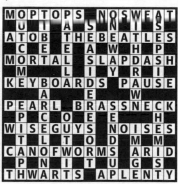

SOLUTIONS

100

```
DOUBLECROSSED
E N A M E T L W
GUTHRIE NERVINE
O H G R O E T S
CRETE YOUNAMEIT
E F N K E
NILOT ROCHESTER
T A O E E R R N
RETINITIS SHIES
I Y U B A
CHAMBERED CZECH
I E L N O R S A
TERRACE GRAMMAR
Y I I E G M A A
HEARTSTOPPING
```

101

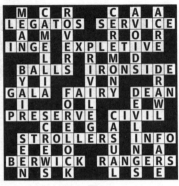

```
M C R C A A
LEGATOS SERVICE
A M V R O R
INGE EXPLETIVE
L R R M D
BALLS IRONSIDE
Y I V N N R
GALA FAIRY DEAN
I O L E W
PRESERVE CIVIL
C E G A L
STROLLERS INFO
E E O U N A
BERWICK RANGERS
N S K L S E
```

102

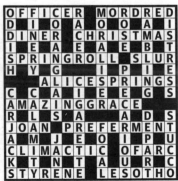

```
OFFICER MORDRED
D I O A O O A I
DINER CHRISTMAS
I E A E A E B T
SPRINGROLL SLUR
H Y G I P I E
ALICESPRINGS
C C A I E E G S
AMAZINGGRACE
R L S A A D S
JOAN PREFERMENT
A M J E O I P U
CLIMACTIC OFARC
K T N T A U R C
STYRENE LESOTHO
```

103

```
CARPARK BOARDER
T R U S I A A
PIKE BEHINDBARS
S E I A K B M
PHONIC KEEPITUP
O O E D N F
BOLOGNESE HAIFA
U P T
SKATE LEAFLETED
N E E A O M
CODRIVER RAYGUN
W W E E E A L
PERENNIALS COAT
T A E N E H T
CHARADE GENTEEL
```

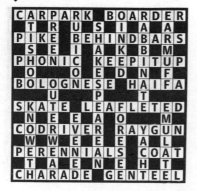

104

```
W D S F C B S T
RAREEARTH ASTER U
E A E I A R R U
NAKED GARDENING
E P I L P
DISCORD ACCEPTS
U T D O E E
COPRA DAY WORLD
K R T A P G
SLIPOFF DRABBLE
C F A R U
TAKESTOCK SISAL
O O T D O L T I
PRUNE INTHEBUFF
E T M L A Y P T
```

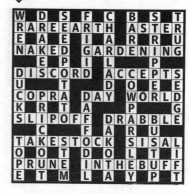

105

```
C M C O H R
HABITUAL DREMEN
P J K A S A P
WEST SERBOCROAT
L O D L I S
TERROR ETERNITY
S O R T G
SOURCE DECAYS
N A S I K
PANDEMIC GADGET
M R I R Y W
RAZORSHARP EPEE
Z B O W S C R
VENIAL LAUGHTER
D N E M O D
```

SOLUTIONS

106

D	I	S	R	E	G	A	R	D		H	O	S	T	S
I		P		S		U		E		O		U		P
S	L	E	E	P	I	N	G	P	A	R	T	N	E	R
C		L		Y		T		R		S		F		I
O	N	L	Y				D	E	R	E	L	I	C	T
		E		A		G		S		W		S		Z
F	E	R	O	C	I	O	U	S		O	C	H	R	E
A				R		L		I		M				R
N	A	C	H	O		D	U	N	G	A	R	E	E	S
T		L		B		P		G		N		X		
A	D	O	R	A	B	L	E				S	P	A	M
S		C		T		A		T		A		O		U
T	A	K	E	I	N	T	O	A	C	C	O	U	N	T
I		E		C		E		P		H		N		E
C	O	D	E	S		D	E	S	C	E	N	D	E	D

107

B	A	Y	L	E	A	F		C	A	T	E	R	E	R
	V		E		L		T		D		M		A	
F	O	A	M		B	L	O	O	D	Y	M	A	R	Y
	C		O		U		A		U		E		N	
M	A	G	N	U	M		D	E	C	A	N	T	E	R
	D				E		I		E		T		S	
T	O	P	B	A	N	A	N	A		W	H	I	T	E
			E				T				A			
S	C	O	L	D		C	H	I	P	O	L	A	T	A
	A		L		S		E		A				A	
C	R	A	Y	F	I	S	H		L	A	R	Y	N	X
	V		A		M		O		E		I		G	
P	E	A	C	H	M	E	L	B	A		O	V	E	N
	R		H		E		E		L		J		L	
B	Y	H	E	A	R	T		D	E	C	A	P	O	D

108

L	A	Y	G	R	E	A	T	S	T	O	R	E	B	Y
O		U		O		U		O		X		N		O
C	O	L	D	W	A	R		P	O	L	Y	G	O	N
K		E		D		A		H		I		A		K
S	O	L		Y	E	L	L	O	W	P	A	G	E	S
M		O		I				C		S		E		
I	N	G	E	S	T	I	B	L	E		I	D	E	A
T				M		R		E		W				U
H	O	S	E		C	R	U	S	T	A	C	E	A	N
		T		E		A				R		M		A
A	R	R	I	V	E	D	E	R	C	I		B	O	T
M		A		E		I		I		N		A		U
A	N	T	E	N	N	A		S	H	E	A	R	E	R
T		U		S		N		E		S		G		E
I	A	M	F	O	R	T	U	N	E	S	F	O	O	L

109

```
A   T H   S C   S   G   M
YAHOO  TRATTORIA  AT
E  R M  R  R O A  T
STEGOSAUR  COPSE
  W    I    O H  H
PROPHET  TEARSUP
E  U  A  E  S    O
PUTIN  NYM  TRICK
Y    D    I  I R  E
SAPIENS  SUCCOUR
  H  D  U    A   N
GROWN  CONTRACTS
O  N  E  K  D E L L
OVERSTEER  AGAPE
N  S  S  R  Y R D W
```

110

```
MASEFIELD   RIME
U  H  R  L  I E  I
ANTELOPE  CLAUSE
R  L  S  C K L  T
TOILET  TRIBALLY
E     O    N L  E
STAYUP  ROSSETTI
H     A    O    O
PENNORTH  NANTES
R  E  A  A    O
REAWAKEN  BETRAY
F  B  E  O  U H N
BROOKE  VERLAINE
O  L  T  E  N L U
EMIT  STRESSFUL
```

111

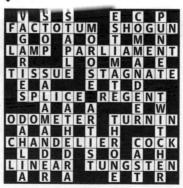

```
V S S      E  C P
FACTOTUM  SHOGUN
G O A  O  T M  N
LAMP  PARLIAMENT
R  L  O  M A  E
TISSUE  STAGNATE
E  A    E  T  D
SPLICE  REGENT
  A  A  A  E  W
ODOMETER  TURNIN
A  A  H  H    T
CHANDELIER  COCK
L  D  D  S O A  H
LINEAR  TUNGSTEN
A  R  A    E T  R
```

SOLUTIONS

112

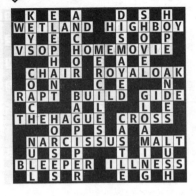

113

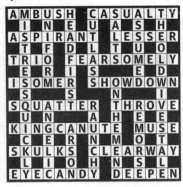

114

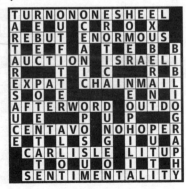